THE 10 C's OF SUCCESS

Success Is A Journey Not A Destination

Published by CelebrityPress®, Orlando, FL.

CelebrityPress® is a registered trademark.

Printed in the United States of America.

ISBN: 978-0-9991714-2-4.
LCCN: 2017958902

This publication is designed to provide accurate and authoritative information with regard to the subject matter covered. It is sold with the understanding that the publisher is not engaged in rendering legal, accounting, or other professional advice. If legal advice or other expert assistance is required, the services of a competent professional should be sought. The opinions expressed by the authors in this book are not endorsed by CelebrityPress® and are the sole responsibility of the author rendering the opinion.

Most CelebrityPress® titles are available at special quantity discounts for bulk purchases for sales promotions, premiums, fundraising, and educational use. Special versions or book excerpts can also be created to fit specific needs.

For more information, please write:
CelebrityPress®
520 N. Orlando Ave, #2
Winter Park, FL 32789
or call 1.877.261.4930

Visit us online at: www.CelebrityPressPublishing.com

THE 10 C's OF SUCCESS

Success Is A Journey Not A Destination

By KEITH M. GILLIES, CFP®

CelebrityPress®
Winter Park, Florida

DEDICATION

All proceeds from this book are going to a cause that is very dear to my heart—The Miracle League. The mission of this organization is to: 1.) Provide opportunities for children with disabilities to play Miracle League baseball, regardless of their abilities; 2.) Promote community support and sponsorship of Miracle Leagues; 3.) Promote the construction of special facilities that meet the unique needs of Miracle League players and their families.

My son, Keagan, promotes a program called "K's for Kids" to raise funds for The Miracle League. If you have a chance, please view the four minute video:

https://vimeo.com/211004977/9b2fa79ddb

For more information on The Miracle League, and how you can get involved, visit: www.gnomiracleleague.org

CONTENTS

FOREWORD

BY JOANN M. MARTIN
CEO, THE AMERITAS COMPANIES

It has been my privilege to know Keith M. Gillies for over ten years. Keith's commitment and dedication to his work and clients, to his family, to his community, and to his country have impressed me. Keith now brings his heartfelt beliefs to us first-hand through his book "The 10 C's of Success."

The 10 C's capture the values, beliefs, and principles that have inspired and motivated Keith on his journey through his productive and fulfilling life. I was inspired, and I believe we can all be inspired, by being reminded of the 10 C's and their potential significance in our lives and the lives of others: choices, commitment, character, charity, creativity, confidence, control, change, competition, and champion. These principles carry enormous meaning and potential for good.

Keith's book speaks clearly to his commitment to the service of others, particularly special needs youth who desperately need and can benefit from our support and help. His book describes how he has helped special needs and disadvantaged youth, as well as more fortunate youth, through his commitment to, belief in, and actions in support of youth sports and athletics.

Keith's love of sports goes back to his childhood. His affection for his alma maters, Tulane University and University of New Orleans, shines through the pages. Keith's book provides a number of real and colorful examples of experiences he has shared with others that have affected his worldview and contributed to his professional, personal, and spiritual growth and journey.

The book contains interesting life-lessons and anecdotes of such historic people as Edward Rickenbacker, Eleanor Roosevelt, Mark Twain, and Winston Churchill. It contains a sprinkling of rich and stimulating quotes from such well-known persons as Dr. Norman Vincent Peale, Peter Drucker, Christopher Morley, Charles Barkley, Napoleon, Thomas Carlyle and Socrates. As one example of a pearl of wisdom, Keith writes that when champions stumble, they:

- Get back up again
- Analyze what went wrong
- Work on getting better
- Wait for their next opportunity
- Take the shot
- Score!

We would all do well to keep this in mind, especially when we encounter difficulties, frustration, hardship, and tough times.

Keith's book caught my interest from the outset, is a fun read, and a good reminder of some of the principles we should strive to live by. Keith, I believe, walks his talk, and our families and communities are better for his contributions to those less fortunate, and his caring service to others.

INTRODUCTION

Success (n): the accomplishment of an aim or purpose.

When we think about successful people, we often look for "the proof in the pudding," in other words, accomplishments. As you read this book, it is my hope that you will gain clarity into success the way I have. In these next Chapters, I'll share with you the 10 C's, which outline how to seek success and gain more value in your life. What you do with that information will be up to you.

A word of wisdom: while the journey of success is absolutely worth taking, it's important to remember one thing: it is a lifelong journey. I wish no one the curse of experiencing all of their successes at a very young age, because there is so much more life to live. Setting high expectations, building a plan to achieve that success, and remaining focused, hardworking, creative, and attentive are all easier said than done.

I couldn't be more excited to share these principles with you, to help you learn how to be successful in work and in life.

CHAPTER 1

SUCCESS AND GOALS

I believe there is a difference between the accomplishment of an aim, and the accomplishment of a purpose. As you read on, you will quickly learn that this is one of the most important parts of this book. I believe the accomplishment of an aim is an ultimate destination, as in a championship. The accomplishment of a purpose, however, means much more. When we base success around a purpose, then our accomplishments occur during the journey.

One of the things I love doing most in my free time is coaching basketball. Witnessing the growth and change in the players is truly inspiring, and contributing my part to our team's success always raises my spirits, even when I am having a rough day.

Every time I step onto that court with the team, I am reminded that success is not just about winning. Sure, championships are nice, but at the end of each season, only one team wins that last game. Does that mean the others failed? Not to me. Measuring success by championships alone forces us to miss out on most of life's incredible lessons. This is why I believe that success is a journey, not a destination.

When I coach, at the end of every practice, at the end of every game, we talk about the journey of success. We review our practice that day and the accomplishments of the season to that point. Goals are destinations. Championships are destinations.

Success, on the other hand, is much deeper.

Sometimes our destinations and our goals are beset by detours. Detours are part of life. We encounter detours while driving, while flying, and on our journeys of success. These detours must not discourage us as we work toward our goals and destinations, as we enjoy our respective personal journeys.

"Shoot for the moon. Even if you miss, you'll land among the stars."
~ Dr. Norman Vincent Peale

Dr. Norman Vincent Peale is someone I had the great privilege of hearing speak years ago. It was one of the greatest joys I have had in my life. Dr. Peale was a minister and author most famous for his book, *The Power of Positive Thinking*, an international bestseller.

During this opportunity to hear him, he talked about some of the wisdom he shared in his book, and paraphrased the quote above, accrediting it to someone else. I was surprised. As it turned out, the quote is more commonly attributed to–and inspired by–Les Brown, an entrepreneur and motivational speaker. The dynamic and accomplished Dr. Peale had many quotes attributed to him, which made it a bit surprising that he would speak of the work of others, and not his own. The answer to what I wondered was soon revealed. Giving credit to others was just the way of Dr. Peale. The simple successes of both the ordinary and the extraordinary motivated him. In turn, he used these examples to motivate many others to success.

So, let me repeat this quote with the correct attribution:

"Shoot for the moon. Even if you miss, you'll land among the stars."
~ Les Brown

All these years later, this quote remains with me. Through Dr. Peale, I was inspired enough to research more about Les Brown.

He began as a sanitation worker who dreamed of going into radio, politics, and ultimately, the motivational speaking arena—a place where you can empower many if you connect with your message. I also learned that Les formed and ran a youth group for underprivileged young men in Miami, Florida. He inspired his charges to dream and accomplish great things, as Les himself accomplished.

Was Les always able to motivate because he was a "well known someone?" No. I can only imagine a teenager in south Florida learning from such a great man. I imagine hearing his booming voice directly, cajoling them to "Shoot for the moon. Even if you miss, you will land among the stars!" Imagine the lives he touched and changed with a simple, but powerful, message.

Les Brown understands our children are our most important resource. With the immense resources of our country (albeit, some misdirected resources), I often wonder why so many schools and families fail to provide the foundation for success to every young person in America. Thank God for people like Les Brown.

Because of what I can imagine, the first source of this quote is irrelevant to me, whether it be Dr. Peale or Mr. Brown. What matters is how it has affected me in coaching, business, and especially in life.

Coaching basketball was a way to help kids imagine just a bit more for their lives. It has always been an avocation that I have enjoyed and I was invested in helping the kids maximize their talents. Through this process over those many years, I believe I learned as much from the players as what I taught them. At the end of each practice, and in the locker room after each game, I reminded them of two things:

1.) Success is a journey, not a destination.
2.) Shoot for the moon. Even if you miss, you'll land among the stars.

Every season I would also invite friends who were successful in business, politics, sports, and education to speak to my players. I wanted them to learn that they could accomplish anything in life if they believed in their own abilities, were disciplined, and worked smart.

Today, I am very proud of many of my former players, several of whom have achieved success in academics, athletics, and life. However, one family stands out in my life—the Hayes family.

Brandy Hayes is a single mom, hardworking and dedicated, the way of many single moms. Her son Brendon was one of my best players. He would often tell me that he believed me when I told him he could achieve anything. He was also a good student due to his efforts, and his mom's persistence, she would not let him fail.

During his 8th grade year at St. Joan of Arc in LaPlace, Louisiana, I encouraged Brendon to attend Brother Martin High School, an all-boys college preparatory high school in New Orleans. I also lobbied his mother to allow Brendon to accept the academic and athletic challenges of Brother Martin. I knew this young man had it in him, and I was compelled to allow him to prove it to himself.

Brendon applied and was easily accepted to Brother Martin. He graduated with honors in 2015 and accepted a full football scholarship to the University of Central Florida. But this is not the end of Brendon's story. He worked hard, but there is another hero—his mother, Brandy.

As a single mom, Brandy figured two things that Brendon needed to attend this school, this wonderful opportunity for him. She:

1.) Had to find a way to pay for Brother Martin.
2.) Needed to figure out how to transport him to a school that was thirty-five miles away from her home.

Brandy made it work, even when it was not easy or convenient. She believed and she inspired her son, just as much as anyone else could have.

I treasure the times I get to spend with Brendon. When he is home from Central Florida, we always make time for lunch. Brendon loves his mom, grandparents, and sister. I am convinced Brendon will have an incredibly successful life, personally and in his career of choice.

Every time I think about the sacrifices that Brandy made, that many parents make, and see how it can have such a profound impact on their child and children, I must work to give my best, consistently.

Today, Brendon's journey is far from over, but I am incredibly proud of his path. Even more so, I have learned so much from Brandy and her love for her son and daughter. They will continue to the greatness they deserve. By all accounts, Brendon has already experienced success and his journey is just beginning.

"You are what you do, not what you say you will do."
~ Carl Gustov Jung

Carl Gustov Jung is famous as an inventor, journalist, psychiatrist, and scientist. His writings influenced many in the fields of the arts, religion, and literature. Carl Jung traveled the world to study many different cultures. His quote above forms the basis for the many who consider him the father of analytical psychology, which is the study of a person from their conscious and unconscious beliefs.

This leads me to the inspiration behind the C's of Success. I am blessed to meet many successful people in my professional career and in my personal life. There are also too many people who talk a good game and fail to deliver. It generally does not take too long to identify such unsuccessful souls. You are what you do; not what you say you are going to do.

In the spring of 2000 my oldest son Blake decided to leave competitive year-round swimming to play other sports. One of those was baseball. He was a tall, strong, and lanky kid. These attributes lead his first coach to think he would make a good pitcher. As a father who wants the best, I wanted to give my input, but I did not. I made it a goal long ago that I would not privately coach my own kids in any sport. Besides, I knew very little about pitching.

Fate stepped in and my son and I were on our way to a birthday party he was attending and there was a "guerrilla marketing" sign in a yard we passed by that advertised pitching lessons. I took down the information and called the number when I arrived home.

The voice at the other end of the number was a wonderful surprise. It was Bob Moreci, a man with a stellar reputation. I could think of no one better to work with Blake.

When Blake showed up for his first lesson with Moreci, I was the one who began to receive an education. I learned that there was much more to pitching than velocity.

Bob said, "Blake, there are four C's to successful pitching: conditioning, concentration, control, and confidence. There is not a 'V' in those four C's, that comes later."

His words caught my attention and I was captivated; partially because I had just embarked on my public speaking platform, mostly to small industry groups. I began to watch and pay attention. At times it was tough, because Blake was not a very good pitcher when he started (He later was a four year letterman in college, as a pitcher). However, Bob's comments regarding the four C's kept swimming around my mind. My conclusion was that if baseball could have four C's, surely I could find a number of C's that related to success in business and life. Thus, *The 10 C's of Success* was born.

The C's have changed my life and perspective profoundly. I chose the ten words in this book that begin with the letter "C" to help explain how I conduct my life and operate my business. They are placed in an order to tell a story from the choices we make to ultimately achieving our personal championship.

From what began as a friend inviting me to Shreveport to speak at a meeting, my opportunities to reach out to others have grown exponentially. Over the past fifteen years, I have refined *The 10 C's of Success* numerous times. With each presentation, combined with my journey in success, I have seen where the message and impact can be improved. It is so exciting.

Today, I have made over one hundred presentations across our great country. Many groups have invited me back, which is pretty encouraging. I am grateful that what I have to say is something that helps enough people that I receive those continued invitations.

This entire concept has now grown to the point where friends suggested that I write a book around the presentation. Like many people faced with the seemingly overwhelming task of writing a book, I have put it off more than turned it on. I have started outlines, set them aside, and then returned to them. However, finally, the book is here. What you have in *The 10 C's of Success*, is the most up to date version of these concepts, and I couldn't be more proud to have the opportunity to share this wisdom on a larger scale. Let this book be useful to you, be it for daily inspiration, outlining a plan, or simply just professional growth.

I recall Bob Moreci just like the day I met him; I will never forget him. He was a good coach and mentor to Blake. Like many good coaches, Coach Moreci used other tools to teach. His was a professional trumpet player and would often bring and play his trumpet to validate a point, usually about training. Blake learned much from him, and those lessons, I believe, have helped him with the challenges his life has brought, many which are addressed throughout this book.

One exciting test in writing this book was finding a way to channel the years of work I've been doing in presentations. While a lot of those stories made their way into this printing, I believe it's important to inject a little levity and personal flare into all that you do.

To give you a flavor for the way I present: I begin with humor, as that helps both the crowd and me to relax, and to set the tone that we are going to have a little fun. Hopefully when I'm warming up the crowd, I'm not just telling corny "dad jokes." However, maybe sometimes I do. Most frequently, I joke about the state I love, Louisiana, and my hometown of New Orleans. One of the early questions I like to ask of the audience when I'm traveling is how many people have visited Louisiana. Of course, many hands go up.

Then I ask how many people have visited my hometown of New Orleans, and invariably, more hands go up. I then remind the crowd that New Orleans is indeed in Louisiana, even though sometimes the state does not claim us; and sometimes we do not claim the state.

Humor, if used properly, is a powerful tool. Think back to the days of jesters who held court for kings. The jester helped break down barriers with humor and was the one person who could do so without his head getting lopped of his shoulders. A definite plus! In Shakespeare, it's the jester or Fool who often has all the answers, but takes a lighter approach to life. The comedian Jerome Silberman once said, "A little nonsense now and then is cherished by the wisest of men." This wonderful comedian and actor is now known as Gene Wilder, a legend in his craft.

One last thing...

As you take your journey through *The 10 C's of Success*, remember to return to the difference between success goals, which are destinations (aims) and the success of a journey (purpose). If you have ever read the book, or watched the movie *Moneyball*, you learn Billy Beane, the general manager of the baseball Oakland Athletics, is still trying to win his last game. No one can deny the success of the Oakland Athletics, because at the end of the day, there is often just:

• One winner
• One elected to office
• One valedictorian
• One champion

That is why I believe success is a journey, not a destination.

CHAPTER 2

TIME FREEDOM & FINANCIAL FREEDOM

Freedom (n): the power or right to act, speak, or think as one wants without hindrance or restraint.

Our freedom is often underappreciated or assumed, which can lead to regrets in life. There are two types of freedoms that lend to our life experience as a whole:

- Time freedom: you have all the time in the world, but no money.
- Financial freedom: you are very successful with work, but your personal life is lacking.

Finding the balance that is necessary between time freedom and financial freedom is not easy, but it is worth the pursuit. My life would be hollow if I only pursued one freedom without the other. Balance is key.

"For most people, the price for security is personal freedom. And without freedom, many people spend their lives working for money, rather than living out their dreams."
~ Robert Kiyosaki

Robert Kiyosaki is the author of the *Rich Dad, Poor Dad* series of books. While I do not agree with all of Mr. Kiyosaki's teachings of finance, one concept we agree upon is the creation of capital assets: assets that create income for clients. Your home is generally not a capital asset, unless you plan on selling the home and converting the funds to capital assets. Capital assets are assets such as 401(k) Plans, Brokerage Accounts, Certificates of Deposit, and other like assets. Getting wrapped up in the money you need to earn to achieve the life you envisioned financially can put you at risk of becoming a workaholic. If that occurs, where is there room for the experiences that life is meant to provide? The word fulfillment means something different to us all, but to me, having a balance of freedoms–time and financial–means everything to me.

It is wonderful to really enjoy your work. I am blessed to fall into that category. I recognize what a privilege it is to connect with a career that fills me with passion and satisfaction. Sure there are stressful days, as well as days when the workload is never-ending. However, what my career has allowed me to do in my life outside of work is truly balanced and exciting.

We all must be considerate of our warehouse of time. What I mean by this is that we each get 1,440 minutes a day. This is time that we cannot recover once spent. We must remain mindful that each and every minute we have is intricately valuable.

What about you? When you are not working, what excites you? Is it a ball game or a concert that commands your free time? Maybe you enjoy golf, tennis, bowling, chess, or reading. Maybe it is just spending time with your family. It is your choice, but what is important is that you make that choice.

There comes a time in life when we are going to reflect on how we invested our time. We must all hope that we see just as many joyful moments with friends and family as those moments we spent behind our desk or committed to our careers.

This is an important topic in my presentations. I often ask my audience to close their eyes and imagine that it is Saturday morning, the kickoff to a weekend (we all love those). What do you want to see yourself doing? I ask you, the reader: imagine you have a whole month of Saturdays to live. Do you want to spend those Saturdays at your office? Or would you like to spend those Saturdays:

- Attending a ballgame?
- Taking your grandchild to a park?
- Enjoying a movie with your significant other?
- Reading a good book?
- Listening to your favorite musician or group?
- Traveling to the beach?
- Cooking and eating your favorite meal?

Far too many people can only see the work, not the joy. They are in a position where they have to play catch-up at the office instead of going out and enjoying what the weekend will offer them. These same people face career burnout, and rely on infrequent and too-short vacations to recharge.

The financial-time freedom trade-offs are real. Creating balance means assuring there is actual balance in your life. To achieve balance, you will also need to consider your loved ones: being a good spouse, parent, grandparent, colleague, and friend. You may choose to invest time in learning a new hobby. Maybe you enjoy volunteering—our communities always need dedicated volunteers. Maybe taking a walk with your spouse will provide the quality time together you both need. The list of what could be an amazing use of your time freedom goes on and on.

These experiences are all so important to me in order to lead a fulfilled life; I cannot imagine my life without them. Creating this balance is most important in our lives; it is worth the time to create the most special memories.

Good news! You can still earn a living and take care of your financial responsibilities and well-being along with creating balance. Not every experience costs money, the only thing you need to do is dedicate the time you need to make a difference in your life and the lives of your family, friends, and colleagues.

Within the concepts of the 10 C's, many of the answers exist for you on how to take steps that lead to both financial freedom and time freedom. It does not matter from where you are starting ... only where you are going.

If you are holding off on your personal dreams to a time after you are at your "best" financially, remember that best is a subjective term. If striving for your personally defined best leaves you missing out on special moments and feeling unfulfilled, then you may want to reevaluate your approach. You will want to consider creating a strategy to shift your priorities around that which is focused upon in the 10 C's. They are meant to help you be of service and to serve the greater good.

CHAPTER 3

THE 1ST C: CHOICES

Choice (n): an act of selecting or making a decision when faced with two or more possibilities.

Christopher Morley is an essayist and journalist who is widely acclaimed as one of the greatest of his generation. He was the son of immigrants who earned the opportunity to study at Oxford College as a Rhodes Scholar. He was a writer for the New York Evening Post and had a bestselling novel, *Kitty Foyle*, in 1939.

> *"There is only one success: to be able to spend your life in your way."*
> ~Christopher Morley

Morley described success as living your life on your terms. He died in 1957, but not before living his life in his way.

Earlier, we reviewed time freedom and financial freedom. For many, to spend a life in one's own way requires both time and financial freedom. While this may sound fairly fantastic, it is a worthwhile exercise to consider how we will spend our lives, especially in our own way. Again, this is what I mean about the purpose, the journey. Making this decision is a worthwhile exercise.

It is funny: we may feel like we do not have the time to make the choices and decisions that bring our lives balance. Sometimes we must choose one thing over another, like the saying goes, "work now" and "play later." However, I challenge you to see that there are other ways. There is one thing that we are assured to have every single day (if we are blessed to have that day): that gift is a warehouse of time, your 1,440 minutes each day. This never changes—no matter what. What we all need to do is decide what choices we are going to make with this warehouse of time.

Our lives are a series of choices, some good and some probably not so good. How do we choose the most preferable parts? How can we make the best choices? Choices have consequences, and that power resides in each of us. We can choose to have no limits and we can choose to overcome adversity. That is the beauty of the ability to choose.

There are a few business choices I have made that turned out to be outstanding. One of those was to bring into my company Luke Trosclair. Luke joining our firm is the result of a tragedy and natural disaster, turned opportunity for us all, which I'll discuss in more detail later in this book.

In late 2005, Luke's (now) beautiful bride, Kristen, worked for me. Kristen is a Certified Public Accountant and she was dating Luke during that time. Luke wanted to be a financial advisor and was finishing his MBA in Finance. Luke's is truly a success story and could warrant an entire book of its own. He lost his father at a young age and was raised, like me, by a single mom. Luke has three brothers and between Luke and his brothers, they earned three advanced degrees.

In the wake of Katrina, Luke was informed that his position with another firm was lost; they had no spot for him. Kristen asked if I would talk to him and counsel him. Of course I agreed. What a wonderful and serendipitous choice. After about ten minutes, I realized this young man had it all. I told Luke I would bring him on as an intern, even though at that time I could not afford to do so. This was one of the best choices I have ever made in my career. Luke is now my friend, my confidante, and my partner. Success is a journey and sometimes the choices we make have profound influences on our lives and careers.

I have two other partners, Mark Cecil and Kim Allen. Mark and I have known one another for over twenty years. I met Kim as he was the incoming chair of the Field Advisory Cabinet of Ameritas, the FAC. The FAC is an advisory group to the senior executives at the Ameritas group of companies, the primary company we represent. Kim called me and invited me to join the FAC. Mark Cecil was then a member of the FAC.

Over the next couple of years, Mark, Kim, and I became great friends. We traveled together, broke bread together, indulged in good wine together, and discussed our businesses together. In 2013, we decided to affiliate our organizations together and another choice, another opportunity developed. We formed United Wealth Advisors Group, LLC.

Our first dictate was: do no harm.

Our second was (and still is): to build an organization that would support our advisors to be the very best they could be; so they could better serve their clients. To that end, we spent hours and hours with our own consultant developing our vision statement.

Our third dictate was: our affiliation was built on the first two, not about our own self-aggrandizement. It was about doing well for the group. Mark, Kim, and I have a conference call every Friday about these very issues and objectives. We now have offices and affiliates in seven cities and we manage over one billion dollars in assets. Yes, we earn more for our families and ourselves, but it is because we made a business choice to be better as a group, not to form a group to only earn more income. It may seem like a fine line–and it is–but we developed a plan and we work the plan. (There will be more to come in subsequent chapters about having a plan.) At the end of the day, it is all about choices we need to make each and every day.

We all choose to seek different goals for all kinds of reasons. Some may choose to be workaholics while others may choose time off. This does not make one an underachiever: it is a personal choice.

I believe the importance is in balance. Without balance, what is the point of any achievement? We can have money and what I call "stuff" without a life, without true balanced success. Balance is the key.

One of the blessings that has come with my success is the ability to travel around the world. One of the most beautiful and relaxing places on Earth that my family and I have experienced is Belize, the sleepy Central American former British colony. This small country has a population of less than 400,000 and it is so beautifully pristine. There have been a few times when we have all thought we may never want to leave. Still, the choice to go always presents itself, and we have taken advantage of this beautiful place many times. Come to think of it, I should have made a trip to Belize to write this book!

We do not really consider ourselves island hoppers, per se, but there are some beautiful islands as part of the country of Belize. On one of our adventures, we visited an island bar just off the coast of San Pedro, Belize. In this quaint, eclectic club, we came across wisdom three hundred feet into the cerulean blue Caribbean. It was a sign that offered a reminder about choice:

"Never get so busy making a living that you fail to make a life."

Wise words from the bar rail of life. I was reminded at this little club that life is about balance and the "Ole 1440." How do we want to allocate our time? If we do not know, we are best served to find out the best ways to allocate our time.

The late great Luther Vandross had a best-selling CD at the end of his life titled *Dance with my Father*. Listening to the title track, we learn that a father has died and the son prays for his mother to have just one more dance with him. If they have this chance, he would choose a song that would never, ever end. This is the point of balance. We can make memories if we make a life and those we love can dance with those memories forever. It is a beautiful thought, as well as concept we are all capable of choosing to create in our lives. Choices have consequences.

One of my very dear friends, Mia Corrente, is the Executive Vice President of a large, regional bank. She is a brilliant person. I hope one day to have the opportunity to work with her—perhaps form a consulting company with her when we both "retire." Mia is a financial genius. Needless to say, she rose through some very tough ranks to her position today. She lost her mom in her childhood. She told me her great aunt, Nonie, who raised her, would whisper in her ear every night, "Make your own way—do not depend upon a man." Mia made the choice to be successful. She works every day on her success. She has earned money for her shareholders and all of the stakeholders in her firm. She is one of my heroes. While she made her own way without needing to rely on a man, balance also means she can have both: Mia also has a wonderful man in her life, my very good friend Scott. They are lucky to have one another.

As I mentioned, I have been blessed. Part of my blessings is to enjoy a career that allows me to control my own time. It was only rarely that I missed anything important for my family. I will hopefully never take that for granted. When you have five kids, that's a lot of love—and time!—to share. It was always my intention to be sure they had the best lives and foundation for their own growth.

When my oldest son, Blake, had a chance to close out an important high school baseball game so our team could make the playoffs, I was there. When he went off to college to play baseball, I had the freedom, both time and financial, to take off Fridays at noon to watch the weekend series. I recognize that privilege and remain forever appreciative of my good fortune for allowing this to be true of my life.

My daughter, Amy played in basketball tournaments every summer. Every chance I had, I was there. My experiences traveling with Amy are some of the best I can recall. Those bus trips from New Orleans to Colorado—now that was something. I recall the time we borrowed a small bus and I drove the team to Tulsa, Oklahoma…in July! Riding on a bus with twelve 18-year-old young, women, now that was something else.

For years we lived on a cypress lake in LaPlace, Louisiana. My neighbor and friend, Dan Mock, was teaching our youngest child, Keagan, to fish. I made it home in time to watch him catch his first fish. I have such fond memories of this time, and can see that first catch still so clearly in my mind.

Two of our other children, Lindsay and Misty, were pretty good tennis players in high school. We were able to make virtually all of those events, regardless of the time or day of the week.

Dance recitals (now that requires special love from a dad like me to be there), athletic events, school events, and many other events, I was blessed to be there. That's what making a life and making memories is all about.

Seek to find balance and avoid the consequences.

Why would we not strive for balance in our choices? The late, great Luther Vandross sang about having one more dance with his father. The choices we make today can decide if those we love will have the indelible memories of all of the "dances" in our lives.

CHAPTER 4

THE 2ND C: COMMITMENT

Commitment (n): the state of being bound emotionally or intellectually to a course of action.

"Unless commitment is made, there are only promises and hopes... but no plans."
~ Peter Drucker

There have not been many ThoughtLeaders®[†] and innovators committed to ways of doing business better than Peter Drucker. He was a writer, management consultant, and university professor, who also worked as an economist and journalist. An accomplished individual, if ever there was one.

With Drucker's commitment to the processes and reasons of why businesses do what they do to be successful, you can gain access to great insight about commitment for you, the professional and the person.

Entrepreneurs are committed people. They have to be. I am often approached with people who have what they think are great ideas. I hearken back to my Tulane days when one of our professors said that good ideas are most often not good opportunities.

One of my sons-in-law is a pharmacist. A few years ago, he approached me with an idea to open his own pharmacy. My first

[†] ThoughtLeaders® is a trademarked term of DN Marks LLC

reaction was how would he possibly compete with the "big boys," the national chains of pharmacies with national distribution and that kind of buying power in the marketplace? I was concerned, not because he asked me to help fund his project (which he did not), but because I was concerned about his success and livelihood. If he failed, how would he support his wife, Lindsay, and their children?

Come to find out, it was not he who failed in this logic, it was me. I failed to understand and see his commitment. A commitment begins by first showing up. The Finnans showed up. He took the risk to open Finnan's Family Pharmacy in 2015. He and Lindsay have continued to work very hard to make it a success and a success it is.

Commitment is a very powerful concept. As we will learn in this book, they had a plan. They developed a business plan, and used imagination and creativity to bring the plan to life. They delivered a product that many consider a commodity and turned it into a service. They had and have a value proposition.

I am very proud of their success, and their success is much deserved. Even someone as brilliant as me can sometimes be wrong, (that is supposed to be funny, even though it is a fact that I can be wrong). Today, Finnan's Family Pharmacy is a continued success.

We can have the best, most honorable intentions, but if we only think them and not act on them, we are not committed to their fruition. Commitment means action. A great reminder of this comes from Calob Leindecker of Baton Rouge, Louisiana. In 2009 he received the Rudy Award, which is given to the nation's most inspirational high school football player.

Calob was in a terrible car accident and people thought he would never play football again. But Calob had a different plan. He amazed his medical team, his family, and his teammates with his commitment to one thing: remaining positive through his rehabilitation. Were their tough days? I am sure there were, but he did not abandon the plan. He vowed to return to the sport that he loved, and persevered through physical therapy and recovery.

The next year his football team went to the state championship again, but this time he was the holder for field goals and extra points. There he was on the field, participating in a big-impact game with his team, a prosthetic replacing where the leg that had been amputated once was. Calob reminds us that when we commit to helping with something in whatever way we best can, we are fulfilling a destination we have at that moment.

Today, Calob is a motivational speaker and he is known for saying: "You can take my leg, but you cannot take my heart."

None of us have to surrender our hearts, regardless of what happens in our lives. Through our hearts we can commit to a great deal and see it through. Calob had a plan and he achieved success.

A few years ago I had the great privilege to meet Mark Keiser. Mark is today someone I consider a good friend. Mark is like Mia Corrente: he is brilliant. And he has more degrees and designations than me! Mark is the Chief Executive Officer of Access Health of Louisiana. Access Health is a Federally Qualified Health Center, FQHC. We could spend hours and chapters on FQHCs, but in its simplified form, FQHCs provide real health care for the needy. We can debate The ACA or Obama Care, but FQHCs do what needs to be done where the rubber meets the road: they provide true primary care to those who most need primary care.

Most communities have health centers. These are places where the neediest in our communities go when they need basic health care. A few years ago, Fred Martinez and Tim Vial, among other community leaders, asked a true expert in health care, Mark Keiser, to help expand the health care center of St. Charles

Parish (Louisiana's version of a county). Mark (of course, a Tulane graduate), agreed to take on the task. He converted the St. Charles Health Center into a FQHC and the rest is history (he is still writing it). They now have over forty locations throughout the gulf south and continue to grow.

With Mark's leadership and guidance, we helped build a recruiting and retention program for Access Health and other community health centers. We now advise the Louisiana Primary Care Association and other health centers on how to recruit primary care providers.

Mark is committed to providing healthcare to those most in need in our communities. He is a good friend, a confidante, and a great American. We need more Mark Keisers in the world. He cares and he puts his talents to the use of the betterment of so many of those who need health care in the Gulf Coast and across the south.*

Commitment is also about involvement. When we are involved we are creating an impact for our betterment and the communities we live and work in, as well. Over the years, I have found that the more involved I am in my community, industry, and with my company, the more success I have. It goes beyond finance and money alone. It involves success in life because I am committed to my role in my life. It is only me who can choose my roles and levels of participation in my endeavors. It is only you who will choose your roles and levels of participation in your endeavors. You control your journey of success.

Regarding participation, the very best high schools strongly encourage their students to get involved in something. At Brother Martin High School's orientation, prior to entering high school, the principal stressed the importance of participation. Maybe it is a club, athletics, drama, or student government, etcetera. Why

---

* Check out this YouTube video highlighting Mark Keiser and Access Health: https://youtu.be/Ca5fKbFzseQ

do they encourage this? When people are committed to and involved in something, it makes a profoundly positive difference in their lives.

The more involved we are, the more focused we learn to be in our vocations.

Why are the very busiest people we know the ones who are asked to engage in the most important of activities in their careers and volunteer lives? It is because they are absolutely focused. There are no wasted efforts and no wasted time in their lives. To make their choices for success, they must be focused.

I believe we have an obligation to serve others as part of our commitment to our community and church. One of my most successful colleagues, Michael Wilcox, often says we must give until it hurts. One of our commitments is to The Miracle League, the charity to which we will donate the proceeds of this book.

It may be hard to believe, but The Miracle League has brought me more little miracles in my life than I feel I could ever contribute to by just giving back, but I sure will love trying. Every person has value and a purpose, regardless of their "disability" or handicap, whether these occurred at birth or later in life. Everyone deserves the ability and opportunity to experience the thrill of competition on some level. The Miracle League helps ensure this happens.

Few things top seeing kids of all abilities–and with such a wide variety of physical challenges–playing baseball and other Miracle League sports. If they are committed, they will expand their skill sets and improve their lives and their journeys. Here are a few specifics:

First, they learn about teamwork. Learning to work as a team member is one of the most important tools a person learns. Secondly, they gain confidence. We will discuss confidence in more detail as one of our C's of Success. Fun is also a very important by-product of commitment and teamwork. If success is a journey, then it needs to be fun. Teamwork, confidence, and fun are all very important parts of enjoying a wonderful sport.

For me, a commitment of my time, enthusiasm, and passion to helping these kids makes me a better person. Their lives gain a profound, fun, and rewarding experience through their commitment to The Miracle League. I have always been involved, but it is different watching these kids. Involvement does not give you the joy of seeing a genuine smile on the face of someone with the challenges of a disability or handicap when they realize that they can do something they may have previously thought of as impossible.

In the spirit of competition, people have opportunities to create healthy changes for themselves and learn important life lessons. Everyone needs these lessons, it is not just a selective club. The champion boxer James J. Corbett penned, "You become a champion by fighting one more round. When things are tough, you fight one more round." That is commitment and that is the state of being bound emotionally or intellectually to a course of action.

CHAPTER 5

THE 3RD C: CHARACTER

Character (n): the complex of mental and ethical traits marking and often individualizing a person.

The complex of mental and ethical traits in this definition deserves discussion. A person very special to me said that one's reputation is what people think of you, but you are your character. Those of high character possess the complex of mental and ethical traits that individualize their personhood and make them who they are in life.

Almost all professional associations have a Code of Ethics. In my professional world, that often means acting in the best interest of another. If we do not act in the best interests of those we serve, then we must have a selfish interest to serve. The best of the best in any sport, profession, or career are those of high character and in business, they act in the best interests of those whom they serve.

Have you ever heard of Eddie Rickenbacker? He was a World War I ace fighter pilot and Medal of Honor recipient with quite an impressive history. He became a pioneer in commercial aviation after the war by becoming the chair of Eastern Airlines. He also took charge of the Indianapolis Motor Speedway, the home of the Indianapolis 500 Motor Race.

For many years I have used his quote:

"The four cornerstones of character on which the structure of this nation was built are: Initiative, Imagination, Individuality, and Independence."
~ Edward Rickenbacker

The cornerstone of our character is everything when it comes to the types of people we are, and how we show ourselves to others. Throughout my career I have observed, counseled, advised, and comforted many very successful men and women. Without exception, these inspiring individuals have all successfully built their lives and careers on their character.

Several of my good friends and clients built their entire company based upon character. EDG is an international engineering company with principal offices in Metairie and Lafayette, Louisiana; Houston, Texas; and Columbus, Ohio. They also have offices in other countries, including Australia. I have often talked with their now retired CEO, Tim Moreau, that the entire story of EDG would make a great Harvard Business School case study. The leaders of EDG embody in their core character many of the chapters of this book. In each chapter, there could be an anecdotal story of EDG.

A few times every year, I visit with Tim. We catch up, and spend time in deep discussions, and he provides guidance to me as well as insights on how to best lead our companies. During these wonderful moments, generally over a few cups of coffee, we discuss business, politics, change, and charity, among other topics. Tim's partners and colleagues have also offered opportunities for me to learn as much from them as they do from me. What is most important is not only the foundation of their company, which is based upon character, but also the belief that there are so many people who will assist us on our journey.

Our character is a sum of our initiative, imagination, individuality, and independence. When these four concepts work together, the qualities that exist within us that reveal our character are formed. Additionally, these are all qualities that are imperative in my role as a financial advisor, both from my perspective and the type of professional I wish to be. It also shapes how I engage with my clients. By knowing their character, and by my clients believing in my character, I can serve clients better with their financial needs.

I would like to break down Mr. Rickenbacker's quote around initiative, imagination, individuality, and independence.

Initiative

> *Initiative (n): the power or opportunity to act or take charge before others do.*

Initiative begins from the moment you wake up in the morning. How do you respond? Are you eager to get going and begin your day, or is the word "snooze" faded off your button from pressing it so much? Or, do you only arise when it becomes "urgent?"

There is a choice that we all have from the minute we wake up in the morning. This is a choice to dictate our own actions.

Perhaps you start out a bit slow, but after that morning cup of coffee and some exercise, you feel the energy growing and you are ready to do what needs to be done—no excuses.

Regardless of how we get going with our day, the important thing is to get going. If you are waiting for someone else to guide and direct you, you are going to be doing a great deal to satisfy the results of their initiatives, but not your own.

What is most important about initiative is that it shows we are willing to put efforts into our results. When this happens, we can more easily recognize any additional skills and training we need in order to become better at what we do.

Imagination

Imagination (n): the faculty or action of forming new ideas, or images or concepts of external objects not present to the senses.

Our imagination helps form our creativity, which is one of the 10 C's. Without imagination, you will find it hard to go anywhere in business or life. Our imagination is what drives us to dream about all those big goals, and I mean "big goals." You aren't just stretching or going out of your comfort level. You are setting crazy exciting, outrageous goals. Those "shoot for the moon," knowing that even if you miss you will be "land among the stars" kind of goals.

We all have the ability to use our imagination to help generate the drive we need to do the things we love, and build the lives we have envisioned. If you are a businessperson, your imagination can help place you in the picture of your success and see the way you will act and feel when you reach milestones. Notice I said "milestones," not goals. Because your goals, remember, are immense. It has been suggested that if you reach a goal, you have not set a hard enough goal. Learning, growing, and doing are all important fuel for our imagination.

When is your best time to imagine? The best time to fire up your imagination is extraordinarily personal: it is not the same for everyone. However, these are the most common ways that most people tap into their imagination, and begin to envision their big pictures:

- Early morning
- Early evening walk
- Bike ride
- Running
- In a creative "zone"
- Other form of exercise

I choose the early morning. My best ideas for creating

opportunities come on those early morning walks. It is when I am most creative and my mind is most open to new possibilities. A fresh day brings me a fresh perspective, and I use that perspective to create.

Individuality

Individuality (n): the quality or character of a particular person or thing that distinguishes them from others of the same kind, especially when strongly marked.

I am concerned that society is forcing us into conformity, which is quite sad considering we all have this amazing, unique potential that is ours to give to the world in some way. This often goes dormant when conformity is forced.

Unfortunately, the old-fashioned idea of debate has succumbed to name calling and the complete rejection of any idea that may be different to one's own. It is not as easy to digress in this manner when we are face-to-face with a person of a different viewpoint, but behind our social media walls or when we can be "anonymous," this kind of behavior is regretfully quite common.

There was a situation I came across one time at a large swim invitation meet for my son. I was helping out, working in the computer room, and there was a dispute. The president of the league came in to help resolve the issue. It was innocent enough, but I said something along the lines of what I felt was the best way to resolve the issue. He corrected me with this response: "That is your idea of the best way to do it: it is not necessarily the best way." He was correct! This is a great point to show how this situation was not a conflict with individuality: that the point is to consider other points-of-view while remaining true to one's self and one's beliefs.

Independence. (n): the fact or state of being independent:
Independent. (adj.) free from outside control;
not depending on another's authority.

Individuality leads to independence.

The tasks of raising our children involve more than just the basic duties we have of ensuring their safety and security. By also teaching children the value of independence, we are giving them an opportunity to explore and learn about the world with more confidence that they can handle themselves. Our baby birds can leave the nest, take flight, and soar high! As we get older, our nest is going to be very crowded if our kids are never independent enough to leave it and use their individuality to achieve great things.

Think of the hilarious movie *Failure to Launch*. The main character refuses to leave home so mom and dad hire a female consultant to, let us say, teach him about independence. In the end it all works out, but along the way–with many funny twists and turns–we learn that independence is important to all parties in a family and in life. Independence makes all of us better.

In My Life

As a financial planner and advisor, I have helped coach many of my colleagues. Teaching these four cornerstones of character, as outlined by Eddie Rickenbacker, has served me well in this endeavor. It is a part of my life and career that I genuinely enjoy on all levels.

These cornerstones have also served me well in my own practice and in leading the directors of our business units. Furthermore, their value has extended to how I can better serve my family, my church, and my community, as well.

Our character is what we are. What we are is formed by initiative, imagination, individuality, and independence.

"People grow through experience if they meet life honestly and courageously. This is how character is built."
~Eleanor Roosevelt

We are a product of those of whom we connect and with whom we engage. One of those people in my life is General Michael Miller, USAF Retired. He is one of the people to whom I look to with the highest of honor and ability. He is a man of God and he is a man of unquestionable character.

General Miller and I met at the University of New Orleans, UNO. UNO was and is a wonderful, high-level educational institution, even as a commuter school. We both had to work to put ourselves through school; a sometimes novel thought these days. We met in class, I believe a night class, and hit it off as friends straight away. The general and his brothers had a roofing company and he worked hard during his daylight hours; I worked as a milkman. Yes, my children are the proverbial children of a milkman.

Between classes we would discuss and debate the issues of the day: the Soviet Union, atomic weapons, Mutually Assured Destruction (MAD, yes, it was madness), and other issues.

One of our classes, coincidentally, was on legislation. We were both Political Science majors and UNO had a highly ranked Political Science department. For this class we had to read a book, *The Dance of Legislation*, which concerned FQHCs, believe it or not. I shared part of this story with my friend Mark Keiser, the CEO of Access Health of Louisiana, which is a FQHC. I highly recommend getting your hands on this book! You will learn how the legislative sausage is made

Sometime in the late 1970s, General Miller and I decided to join the Air Force. We both went through the entire ordeal, going to a recruiting office, reviewing brochures, talking to the recruiters. At the end of the day, I decided against signing up, but Michael did sign on. He joined the Air Force and was accepted into the Missile Launch Officer program. He had his finger on the button, or as he says, he had one of the keys (and I hope I am not getting him into trouble).

As I said, General Miller is brilliant, much smarter than me. He spent part of his career in North Dakota and my family visited him and his beautiful wife, Susie, in Grand Forks. He could not tell me much of what he did, but I enjoyed traveling to meet him and playing basketball until the early morning hours, often it was still light outside.

Michael's career took various twists and turns, but he ended up in hospital administration. That led to a couple of stints in the Pentagon. He earned his star and became the Chief of Staff to the Surgeon General of the Air Force, as a non-medical general officer.

I had the great privilege of attending his induction as a General Officer in Washington, DC with two of our children, Amy and Blake. He also guided Amy, Blake, Keagan, and me on many subsequent visits, on tours of the Pentagon. Imagine that! My friend, General Miller, took us on tours of the Pentagon. I once mentioned to him how proud I was of him on one of these tours. He said, in his usual humble way, that a one-star at the Pentagon was not a big deal. It was a big deal for us! When he retired, I had the great honor of attending that ceremony as well, in Dallas, Texas.

General Michael Miller is one of the most honorable people I know. He is a man of incredible character. As I stated earlier, someone I respect always told me, "Your reputation is what others believe you to be; your character is who you are." General Miller is a man of character. He worked his way through school as a roofer to become one of the most powerful leaders in our military.

Today General Miller is the CEO of a high tech firm near Dallas, Texas. The work they are doing will change the world, for the better. Their projects are highly confidential, but under his guidance they will see their dream to fruition.

My last story about character involves my mom. You will learn more about her later. As you already know, she was a single mom and a great mother. She, my grandmother Amy, and my Aunt Mona Roussel are three of the most influential and foundational people in my life.

When I was young child, my mom took us on the bus to Canal Street in New Orleans with my grandmother Amy. Canal Street was the then equivalent of a shopping mall. All of the best stores were on Canal Street (actually, today this is still the case). It was a treat, a huge treat, to go to Canal Street.

Well, I was a typical young idiot. We spent the day "shopping"—I put that in quotes because we had no money, so it was window-shopping more than it was anything else. However, we made the glorious trip. On the way back home on the bus, my mom discovered that I had shop-lifted a small, insignificant item. She immediately turned us back on the next bus so I could return it. It was a day I learned about choices and character. I had to embarrassingly apologize to the clerk and return the item. She let me know when I returned home about my mischievous action. I can promise you that never happened again.

In 2013, I was honored with the prestigious Lester A. Rosen Humanitarian Award by Ameritas. I recounted that story. My mom says she did not remember that occurrence, but I surely did. I wanted our children to know the character of my mom, so I told the story, however embarrassing to me, from the main stage.

I hope these anecdotal experiences of my great friends and me have an impact on you, and how you choose to spend your time pushing towards goals and life. The choices we make and the experiences we learn impact our character for many years.

CHAPTER 6

THE 4TH C: CHARITY

Charity (n): the voluntary giving of help.

There is a wonderful book written by Bob Burg and John David Mann entitled, *The Go-Giver*. It is a short book with a big message that I highly recommend to clients and friends alike. What really resonates with me in this book is how Burg and Mann created a powerful parable that emphasizes the philosophy that I hope to inspire others with through the *10 C's*.

The main character in the book is a salesman named Joe. He is a go-getter, but like many salespeople, he has hit a wall. In order to survive, Joe seeks out someone who he believes will show him the quick and easy path to success. Yet, what he learns is not what he expects, including how charity can change his life.

This chapter echoes that sentiment: Giving of yourself in service to others has more power than you can imagine. You find the joy in giving just for the sake of giving, but the rewards that you receive back are more significant than you could ever guess. You have to actually give to understand how positive and beneficial it is for you. Enough of that plug, but be reassured—read that book and you will be changed.

> *"We make a living by what we get, we make a life by what we give!"*
> ~ Winston Churchill

Winston Churchill, Sir Winston Leonard Spencer-Churchill, is one of history's great statesmen. He is well known as the leader of Great Britain as its Prime Minister during World War II. Of lesser note is the fact that he won the Nobel Prize for Literature, not for one work, but for his lifetime and body of work. He also overcame a speech impediment to become one of the greatest orators of all time.

Giving is an amazing trait. I believe it is important to give of our time, skills, and treasure for the greater good. If we are not willing to give of these things we cannot truly invest in our families, communities, and our churches or professions. The return is so much more than what may first be perceived as a "sacrifice"...a sacrifice of time...a sacrifice of skills...a sacrifice of our treasure.

For over thirty years I coached pre-teens and teens. It was not uncommon for my friends to question why I gave so much of my time without payment. With busy schedules and so much to do, it just did not make sense to them. We are all busy people and have things to do. What my friends did not understand was really a misperception. They perceived payment as monetary rewards. However, the rewards I received for coaching were largely greater than money could ever satisfy.

At the writing of this book, I am president-elect of the National Association of Insurance and Financial Advisors, NAIFA. It takes a lot of my time and that is without question. However, I feel (and believe) I have learned so much from so many people that without it, my career and business would only be a fraction of what it is today without the NAIFA organization.

Consider this: I travel around the country and have the opportunity to visit with the best and brightest in our profession. Regardless of how high your level of success rises in your career, you can always learn something from anyone, if you choose to take the opportunity. This motivates me, inspires me, and reminds me why I love giving of myself to others. Everyone benefits.

Our current Chief Executive Officer is the amazing Keven Mayeux. Kevin is an attorney by education, but he is an association executive by career. He is bright, articulate, and an incredible leader. As president-elect, he invited Paul Dougherty (our president) and me to a three day CEO symposium sponsored by his professional association. Not only was this training important for my volunteer role, I learned many techniques to apply in our own businesses.

While I only briefly mentioned Paul Dougherty, he is an example of the value of service and serving. Paul is an outstanding State Farm agent. The other members of our Executive Team at the time of this writing are Jules Gaudreau, CEO of the Gaudreau Group in Massachusetts; Matt Tassey, Principle of E.A. Scribner Insurance Agency in Maine, and Jill Judd, another outstanding State Farm agent in California. The time we spend together is amazing and is of great value to my firm and my family.

In the fall of 2008, an acquaintance phoned me to ask if I would serve on the Field Advisory Cabinet (FAC) of the Ameritas group of companies. That person is now one of my very best friends and one of my partners in business. As I mentioned in the Choices chapter, together, we joined with another FAC member, Mark Cecil, to form United Wealth Advisors Group, LLC (UWAG) in 2013. Today, we have affiliates in seven cities and collectively manage over a billion dollars of clients' wealth, while serving thousands of individual savers as advisors to over two hundred retirement plans. Together we find economies of scale, create better processes and systems, and serve more of our communities. Without our collective willingness to serve and spend that volunteer time together, UWAG would not exist. We met and became friends and business associates as a result of serving others.

We encourage service from our teams as well. My business partner in our New Orleans and Little Rock affiliates, Luke Trosclair, is very involved in our professional association, currently serving on our state board and is past president of our local chapter. My son Blake currently serves as our local president and is very much involved in our efforts with The Miracle League.

I could write pages and pages about the people I have met through my service to others, but suffice to say, I have received exponentially more than I have given. Just in measurement of my friendships, my minor donations returned to me so much more. The time spent with Linda Ray, Dean Macheras, Rob Eddy, Elli Blaylock, Donnie Bacque and many others, can never be repaid.

Giving is not just about giving of your time to professional causes that help you; it is also about giving back to the community.

I am so proud of our children, and believe they are ingrained with a sense of giving. We have been involved in many community activities, including our church, the New Orleans Children's Hospital, and most recently, The Miracle League. From what you've read so far, you understand how this organization inspires me.

Are you wondering how I ended up choosing The Miracle League? There are many amazing charities out there that are worthy of time and devotion as a "giver," but this one resonates greatly with my entire family.

My two sons, Blake and Keagan, were baseball players at Brother Martin High School in New Orleans. Both went on to play college baseball, with Blake graduating with three letters from Huntingdon College in Montgomery, Alabama. Keagan is currently a sophomore pitcher at Tulane University in New Orleans. My sons had the wonderful experience of having a high school head coach, Mark Wisniewski, known as Coach Wiz to friends and colleagues. He is not only a wonderful coach, but also a wonderful human being.

Coach Wiz started a program at Brother Martin to raise money and awareness for The Miracle League of Greater New Orleans. Each summer, the athletics program at Brother Martin, led by the baseball team, hosts the Miracle League Day at the school. It is a day that leaves a lasting and profound impact on you—no matter the toughness of your exterior. There is nothing that will touch a heart like watching these very special children play baseball.

These special needs children teach outstanding athletes about the true nature of sports and the game of baseball. It is powerful!

This power affected our youngest son, Keagan, more than the others. He approached me to assist him with a way to raise more money for this important community program. Together we developed the "K's for Kids" program. He presented it to Coach Wiz and he loved the idea. The program is simple:

> For every strike out the staff earns, people pledge an amount of money. It could be a penny, nickel, quarter, dollar, or more. That first year, the program raised over $10,000 for The Miracle League. He hopes to receive permission from the NCAA to bring this program to Tulane, but it still exists at Brother Martin High School.

There are many things that I am excited about with this program, aside from what I have already stated. In specific, I love how it demonstrates that we can take things we enjoy and which we are talented, helping others experience a taste of what it is like to do those same things.

With "K's for Kids" it was also especially fun because our entire family got involved (and still are). Our office helped manage the program; my friends, colleagues, and family across the country donated to the program. It is truly inspirational. Because of Keagan, Coach Wiz, and the wonderful special kids and leaders of The Miracle League of New Orleans, we are donating all proceeds from the sale of this book to the program. Even a single penny to help them is good, and God-willing, I can raise a few more cents than that.

In an excerpt one of Sir Winston Churchill's greatest speeches, he states:

> **"Never give in. Never give in. Never, never, never—in nothing, great or small, large or petty—never give in, except to convictions of honour and good sense. Never yield to force. Never yield to the apparently overwhelming might of the enemy."**

This speech was delivered to the Harrow School in 1941. Of course, it was delivered in consideration of the war and the bravery of the citizens of Great Britain. However, these words certainly apply to much of life, including the good sense and honor of these precious children who are members of The Miracle League.

> **Giving is contagious and it is not always about money, although money is important. However, you must always remember—do not give to receive, give to give.**

I hope this chapter proves the point about the contagion of giving.

CHAPTER 7

THE 5TH C: CREATIVITY

Creativity (n): characterized by originality and expressiveness; imaginative.

The city of New Orleans, "The Big Easy," is filled with a certain mystique: countless tales have been written about her uniqueness. Unfortunately, many of the beautiful accounts written about this fair city lie dormant, no longer discovered by avid new readers. You see, they were written in a time when words did not have to be weighted so heavily. The debate about whether or not times have changed really matters not. What I focus on is the loss of wonderful pieces of fiction that focused the imagination of so many artisans, writers, and just plain characters.

> *"You cannot depend on your judgment when your imagination is out of focus."*
> ~ Mark Twain

Mark Twain is such a character. Born Samuel Langhorne Clemens, Mark Twain was the gifted author of fiction and a legendary humorist. William Faulkner (the writer and Nobel Prize Laurette of Oxford, Mississippi) called Mark Twain the father of American Literature. His classic tales included characters along the great Mississippi River. His two greatest works, *The Adventures of Tom Sawyer* and its sequel, *The Adventures of Huckleberry Finn* are classic novels. Some consider the latter as the great American novel.

Mark Twain loved technology and science. He invested heavily in a printing technology of the time and lost almost all of his wealth. He was encouraged to file bankruptcy and did. However, aside from being imaginative and creative he was a man of character, thus he embarked on a worldwide lecture tour to repay his creditors, while under no obligation to do so.

I always have used Mark Twain as an example of imagination and its importance. When we look at creativity as it's defined, it is easy to see great value in being an original: capable of self-expression and imaginative thinking. Most of us would like to possess these qualities, and even if we deem that we do not, we like the thought of it.

When we think of imagination and creativity and their major roles in our journey, let us not forget the wisdom contained in the words of Mark Twain, embedded in the aforementioned quote about judgment and imagination. It is here we can tap into some of his greatest insights. They are every bit as true today as they were at the time written.

I see great value that can help all of us today, both in our personal and professional lives. Imagination must remain a thriving part of our world to keep the dreams and aspirations of everyone alive, with spirit, desire and with hope.

> *"Curiosity about life in all its aspects, I think, is still the secret of great creative people."*
> ~ Leo Burnett

Leo Burnett was an advertising executive who created the company that bears his name. His creative genius led to some of the most memorable advertising campaigns for all time. These include "Tony the Tiger," the "Marlboro Man," and "The Friendly Skies," which is today still used by United Airlines.

We must allow our imagination to take focus so we can imagine our possibilities. Without creativity, focus and imagination, we are subject to tunnel vision. We must always remain curious, and allow our teams to remain curious.

In business, companies are always at risk of becoming too bureaucratic as they keep the power of imagination in check. They begin to put people into tight boxes that are not natural fits; no longer allowing their greatest assets—their employees—to use their judgment to strengthen and improve business, service, and value on all levels. This places the service and value of the business, along with the employees, in difficult positions. Imagine... there is no acceptance of creativity to solve any particular challenge, crisis, or even answer a simple question. This places companies, and the service to clients and customers, in difficult positions ruled by "what is in the book" and 'we have always done it that way." The leadership of the company or entity has placed their firm in this difficult bureaucratic mess. Free your teams to use their imagination and creativity.

In our company, we have committed to a different approach. By focusing on acceptance of creativity and imagination in our work environment we are able to create distinction. Sure we have processes and systems as an organization and we cannot operate without such guidelines. However, they are guidelines. Every team member has the authority of their own creativity to solve challenges and answer questions. We must find solutions that are logical and not restricted by the phrase "because that is the way we do it." We must reduce apologies for "wanting to do something" but "not being able to," as that is an insane customer service model.

Thus, limitless thinking is an asset, just as much as the minds that are enabled to do it for our business are assets. Yes, we are highly regulated and we do need to pay the utmost attention to these regulations, because to do otherwise would be foolish. Using creativity and imagination is not bending or breaking the rules; it is looking beyond the box—the basics—and into a new level of thinking. It is looking at the rules and regulations to see how we can better serve and gain advantages in the marketplace. It is as exciting as it is fruitful for all of us, on every level.

As we grow, throughout our company it is important to focus on this empowerment more than ever. We have created growth that is based on empowering our entire team to make decisions, at their appropriate level of expertise. Sometimes someone will decide to do something completely differently than I would choose based upon the same facts, but a decision has been made and we have to support the team member who made it. This is far better than the alternative. For example:

A customer or coworker asks, "How come we do this that way?" And the best answer they receive is, "Well, that's the way we have always done it."

That type of boxed-in thinking drains me personally, and also does little-to-nothing to build up a business with employee-fueled power. You know what? Just because something is written in a book does not make it right.

Some of us work in industries or professions with necessary hard and fast guidelines that must be followed—no exceptions. The question then becomes how we can be creative when we are thinking about how to do things within the guidelines? How can we still differentiate ourselves by use of our imagination or our creativity? The answer, of course, is that we can do just that. It is often just a question of a common sense approach to an issue.

It has become easy to just brush things off due to a lack of effort or just a learned behavior within a certain culture. What greatly disheartens me about this is how it naturally snuffs out imagination and all the wonderful benefits that come with it. Our employers may owe us certain things, but we also owe it to ourselves to do great things with our opportunities.

What about attitudes in our workplace? Do we consider the attitudes of our co-workers or our employees? Let us revert to Mark Twain, who also said, "Do not go around saying the world owes you a living. The world owes you nothing. It was here first." This saying resonates deeply with me today. We all know people who walk around with a black cloud over their heads. Their failures are always the fault of others or some indescribable barrier. Stay away from these people. They will do all they can to prevent you from achieving your success.

To myself, and many others, from what news stories sound like, some Millennials and Gen X people really have a challenge on their hands. Too many feel they are owed certain things "just because." Somehow what they want is a given right, not an earned benefit. Please do not misinterpret what may be an overgeneralization, but it creates quite the spark when you contrast the general actions of the newest generations against older generations. Overall, there are some clear differences as the "greatest generation," my generation's parents, were more than willing to work diligently for everything they had in order to make things easier for their heirs. While I am not a mind reader, I am fairly certain they did not envision that success is derived without effort and hard work. Their hopes were that it might be a bit easier for others to use their imaginations and achieve great things as a result—an appreciated opportunity, if you will, from their sacrifices.

This belief, or narrative, is important. We do live in a country that was built upon the idea of sacrifice and effort for success. We were built upon initiative, and when we go around thinking we are owed something we will not have that successful journey. If we believe the world owes us something, we hearken back to Mark Twain's words, "The world owes us nothing; it was here first." That wait may last forever and bring no satisfaction.

You have to be willing to compete to be successful.

We want everyone to always offer their best efforts and receive the rewards of such efforts, but the reality is that not everyone will get a trophy. I see too many participation trophies, awards for last place, and so on. We all know the drill. Life is not that way. Some will do better than others, and as far as I know, there is no formula to gauge who put in the most effort—hours, imagination, vision, and implementation—to see why things turn out the way they do.

The "best of the best" have had plenty of setbacks on their way to their successes. What set them apart was that they did not take comfort in setbacks because someone told them "good job." They saw it as an opportunity to learn from, and then they tap into their creativity to make sure they did not repeat the same mistakes or decisions. They worked harder on their jump shots; their chipping game; their style and content in proposals.

I love the movie Trouble with the Curve. There are so many life lessons in that movie. (Beware, spoiler alert coming.) One character is the egotistical Bo Gentry, the supposed high school phenomenon. We have all seen his type, the "me, me, me" personality. Another is Rigo Sanchez, a true phenomenon, as the humble, hard-working student who is not allowed to play baseball because he made a "B" in Chemistry. How many parents today would do that? Bo gets the big contract; Rigo is discovered; and Rigo takes down big, bad Bo at a tryout for the Atlanta Braves. Both worked on their games, but Rigo's attitude and perseverance led to his success. There was a pivot point in his life and he took it.

I believe pivot points are important, particularly in my profession. The pivot point action requires listening to the client, or potential client, to learn what is important to them. When that is learned, it is important to pivot to illustrate to the client how our firm can help the client achieve his or her goals. The best people I know in business have the ability to pivot. When you talk, you seldom learn anything new – aside from a personal revelation, perhaps

– but when you listen, a stream of new ideas can be absorbed if you allow yourself to be the sponge. These ideas can help you see more clearly and determine a better route to success. The kind where you actually earn your accolades!

Look at it this way, if you want to build a house and tell the architect that you want three showers in your home and they have a plan that calls for two bathtubs that architect needs to master the pivot. They must be able to explain to the customer how they can give them three showers, not two. The satisfied client/customer is all that is important.

In my work as a financial planner the ability to pivot is essential. If you are not talking about what is important to the client you may not have one for long. This is how you build rapport and trust.

Once there is trust you have the ability to come back and help clients understand why there are other things they need to consider on top of what they initially stated. As the expert, people want to hear what you have to offer them, but they do not automatically want to have their requests, or what they believe they desire, disregarded. No one wants to be treated that way. It is disrespectful and void of the imagination.

There is this wonderful Daniel Leather's advertisement that used to run on TV that shows this beautiful woman who is in the lobby of a hotel dining room by herself. She is doing some work and this guy looks at her and makes eye contact. Then he walks up to her and drops his key off on her table.

She looks at him, picks up the key, and smiles. He walks toward the elevator and she gets up and drops off the key to this old guy sitting at another table. He looks at her and picks up the key right away. He walks over to the elevator and gets in.

Once in the elevator, the young guy looks over at him and notices the number on the room key. His excitement suddenly takes a turn.

Now that is a woman who knows how to pivot!

CHAPTER 8

THE 6TH C: CONFIDENCE

Confidence (n): a firm belief in one's powers, abilities, or capacities.

It is important to state that confidence is not to be mistaken for cockiness: they are two completely different things. When you have confidence, you have faith in your ability to do what is required of you in your endeavors. Confident people do not need to tell people how great they are: they illustrate their success with their actions.

"Optimism is the faith that leads to achievement. Nothing can be done without hope and confidence."
~ Helen Keller

Helen Keller was once asked if there was anything worse than losing her eyesight. Her reply was, "Yes, the only thing worse than being blind is having sight but no vision." Helen Keller had amazing perseverance and confidence: she was born deaf and blind, but learned how to communicate and grew into a very accomplished and historical person. A noted author and lecturer, Keller was the first blind and deaf person to ever earn a college degree.

When you reflect on the obstacles life presented to Keller, and the endurance it took for her to overcome her circumstances, it brings new meaning to the quote above about having hope and confidence. Yet, how did she learn to be so confident? Look no further than the story of Anne Sullivan.

Anne Sullivan was nearly blind due to a childhood infection, but she persevered and earned a degree from Perkins School for the Blind. Upon graduation, Ms. Sullivan was approached to assist with a young deaf and blind girl who was prone to temper tantrums. She headed south and met none other than a young Helen Keller. With her guidance, and Helen Keller's intellect, she was able to teach young Helen to sign (sign language) and speak. Helen Keller's confidence and optimism derived not only from her own efforts, but also from the efforts and leadership of her team: her parents and the influential Anne Sullivan.

A modern example of confidence can be found in super athletes such as Payton Manning, Derek Jeter, Michael Jordan, Drew Brees, and Serena Williams They work hard to master their sport so they can have confidence that they will be able to perform when it is required, consistently. You will never hear these athletes brag about how great they are (or were). They acknowledge their teammates as being key contributors to their success, and stay humble when acknowledging their own talents.

Their confidence is built by the teams they have, their coaches, managers, family, and others. They realize that a super athlete is not much without the other players, the team. They realize the team is not much without the league. Finally, they realize the league is not worth much without the fans. It is a system of success.

Super athletes have something in common with superstars in business: both have incredible work ethics and they understand the concept of a team. The stories of inspiration about certain athletes are endless. Not so widely known are the stories of others not in the public spotlight. Most of us have heard about Michael Jordan and his incredible work ethic to gain confidence to perform on an elite level. Two athletes I find noteworthy examples of impressive drive and confidence are Wayne Gretzky, and Charles Barkley.

Wayne Gretzky is a rare person who understood what it took to be a competitor from a very early age. He grew up watching hockey with a pencil and paper in front of him. Gretzky would trace every move that puck made on paper to understand how it reacted and responded to every stick at every angle. They say he did not even look down at the paper—eyes on the screen and pencil to the pad.

"The meek may inherit the Earth, but they never get the ball."
~ Charles Barkley

Finally, there's Charles Barkley. Barkley was an elite professional basketball player and a rare case of a guy who could talk the talk and walk the walk. In college, he was known as the "round mound of the rebound," using his body style to his great advantage. He was the prototypical competitor.

As a talker, Barkley is known for a great many quotes and sayings, and many of them are a dream for a former basketball coach and motivational speaker like me.

I can reflect back to the end of basketball practice, where we would line up the players on a baseline under a goal. We would ask, "Who wants the ball?" It was fun to watch the younger kids ducking and diving to get out of eyesight: of course, those are the very ones we called upon to take the last free throw of practice. Make it, and practice is over. Miss it and it is another suicide (a suicide is a drill where players run from under one goal to the other, while stopping to touch all baselines in between). We wanted this exercise to emulate the need to make free throws at the end of any game, so we continually asked the question in the words of Barkley: "The meek may inherit the earth?" Then, we awaited the answer, "But they never get the ball."

On our team every person needed to have the confidence late in the game to make the shot. In your role, whatever that role may be, do you want the ball?

Through competition, we receive the inspiration to be our best; doing the things we love most.

There is a great lesson in regards to competition and finding a healthy confidence. When it comes to basketball, you have to be able to run in order to play the sport. Players need stamina. It is unavoidable. Without running, you will never be able to finish the game. So, our end-of-practice drill accomplished multiple goals: physical endurance, building confidence, teamwork, practice, and emulation of situations.

Every career has something that is demanded of you in order to be confident to compete. It all comes down to doing what is necessary to get better. During basketball practice, we did what was necessary to get better, we just tried to make it fun for the team.

Getting better does not have to be tedious—it can be fun.

The way you gain the confidence to take the last shot, make the critical pitch, or even the "big catch" all begins with the desire to have the ball. Now, relate this metaphor to your career, whatever that looks like for you at the moment. When the boss comes in the room and says they have a project and they need someone to run it, you want to be the one to raise your hand. By doing this, you are showing you are not the meek, but the confident leader who is willing to make something happen. This drive and assertiveness is the heart of confidence.

Confidence is synonymous within the efforts of many entrepreneurs. To succeed, entrepreneurs must have a different mindset. I am very fortunate to know many successful and inspiring entrepreneurs. To connect the lessons we learned earlier in this chapter—from Hellen Keller to Charles Barkley—let me close with the stories of one successful firm. Derryl Walls, and his two partners, Keith Jackson and Richard Armond, are just, on the surface, ordinary people. Walls, Jackson, and Armond were colleagues in a refrigeration company who decided to embark on their own adventure.

This is a warning to all business owners. Protect your best employees. Make sure they do not become your greatest competitors.

I met them twelve years ago to help with some business planning. With Walls as CEO, the company wanted to invest every dollar back into their company. That confidence paid off in the long run: today, their company is worth millions of dollars, and they have zero debt. They had the confidence to risk everything to build something one of a kind.

Gaining confidence means taking advantage of the resources available to you and using them to their utmost ability to gain new skills so you can be fearless in demonstrating your confidence.

"Stan the Man" Musial was a pro baseball player who was primarily an outfielder and first baseman. He played in the days when they did not have DVDs and digital recordings that you could stop and start as you took notes. It was tape back then, and committing to reviewing tape was a time-intensive process.

What Stan did to gain the self-confidence he needed to say, "I want the ball" was study tape… after tape… after tape. He memorized the speed that every pitcher in the league through each type of pitch—fastball, curveball, slider, and others—and knew how the pitch would react thirty feet from the plate.

He was one of the best in the game during the prime of his playing career; demonstrating an incredible amount of confidence every time he was given an opportunity. But truly, it was the work between games that contributed to his amazing success. It was not easy to get that information and he was resourceful to ensure he had it. What Musial did are things we can all do in any aspect of our lives if we wish to perform with the utmost of confidence.

Stan Musial also said, "I love playing this game of baseball. I love putting on the uniform." We are all better served in life, and in gaining confidence, if we are working in something that we love to do. The hard work and results gain so much more meaning. This is why I ask my audiences during presentations this question: "When you wake up in the morning, do you want to put on your uniform?" Whatever your role is in your organization, you should love putting on your uniform, whether it is a suit, a work uniform, or a player's uniform. If not, then it may be time to look for another career.

You have to be ready to attack your day and be confident in it.

I have found that the best way to prepare for every day is to follow this simple guideline: yesterday I prepare for today. I know that if I start my day off knowing what I have to do, I will be better prepared to act in confidence and react with agility to whatever surprises may come my way. Surprises happen to all of us, but with preparation comes confidence and the ability to manage the certain disruptions and challenges of everyday.

Yesterday I prepared for today. And before I leave today I will prepare for tomorrow so that in the morning when I wake up I am ready, I know what must be done. This is how you gain confidence to put on that uniform

Confidence also requires mastering mechanics, which is the most tedious part of gaining confidence that most of us will ever encounter. My sons are baseball pitchers and with that comes a necessity to master the mechanics. If you do not, you will get sore, risk injury, and not perform at the highest competitive levels.

Through mechanics we are all able to maximize our God-given abilities.

We need the proper mechanics to be confident in business, as well, and I think too often we do not stop and take time to educate ourselves to get better at whatever we do. Every occupation has certain "mechanics" to it. Again, it is boring and not the most fun you can have, but investing time in refining your career will help you excel at a rate that would not otherwise happen.

In basketball practices, we emphasized mechanics by using skill stations. Everyone is required to work at every one of them. Examples of what we may do include having someone practice weak-handed layups. It is hard to do and it requires a lot of focus and self-awareness to grow competent and confident at this skill. However, it is worth it, because during a game that may be the skill necessary to convert an important basket. When the opportunity arises, you are prepared to contribute to your team confidently.

With your career it may be memorizing regulations, rules, and details so you can be more proficient in your assessments. Perhaps it is taking on that extra project that will give you entry into a dream project you are striving to achieve. Role playing helps. Observations of those who are better than you will also help build a knowledge base. We can learn much from others. Do not fear asking for assistance. Knowing the mechanics of what is necessary to excel is critical to developing confidence.

Whether you are attacking a basket or a new project at work, being masterful in your mechanics will increase your confidence that you will succeed.

Are there times when we will miss that shot, or miss the mark on the project? Yes, there are, but the confident competitor returns to their "mechanics" to smooth out and overcome those failures. Overcoming the emotions and disappointments when things do not go as we hoped (or planned) is important. It gives us the resilience to keep applying our best efforts. We must allow ourselves to fail magically while we seek success wonderfully.

I have a friend who is not in the spotlight and headlines. His name is Bobby Gravolet, Jr. He is a river pilot today, but it was not easy to earn that rare, elite position. If you are not from an area that is near large rivers or other crowded waterways, you probably have never paid attention to river pilots, but they have probably crossed your path at some point. For example, if you have ever vacationed on one of those enormous cruise ships, you can bet at one point a pilot was directing and navigating that vessel. Also, know this—it is not easy to become one. You have to pay your dues, which means working on merchant ships for years in order to get an opportunity to sit for the test.

When you are lucky enough to pass the test, you move on to be voted in by the existing pilots association. If you are not a part of a family of pilots, it is even more difficult. Gravolet was confident that he could do it, but he knew that he had to do more to prove it to everyone else. He did this by going to the riverbank every morning when he was not working to greet the pilots and introduce himself. He also did this on his days off and in his free time. He was committed that these guys would at least know who he was and what he was all about.

All of Gravolet's hard work finally got him to the point of a vote. His colleagues began the voting and even with his hard work and dedication, his first vote was still a "no." Most would say he did all he could do. He illustrated confidence, was creative, was (and is) a person of high character. Still, after that first vote, even though he did all he could do to earn his deserved spot that was not the way it played out.

Bobby Gravolet went back to work and kept doing what he felt would give him his best opportunity and chance to reach his goal. Finally, he was voted in. Without mastering mechanics and developing confidence that he deserved that coveted spot, would it have ever happened?

There are a handful of people like Bobby Gravolet in this world who are willing to do whatever is necessary to achieve a goal or dream. Their stories will never be known on a national or global basis, but they are inspirations. They are great mentors and people to notice, for a little initiative and imagination can do wonders for your confidence.

Take a few moments to think about what you can do to show your confidence in your chosen career or path. Resumes are a dime a dozen and limited in what they can reveal about you. While necessary, it is more important to prove what you can do and how you are unique. Put yourself out there. How can you channel your inner Wayne Gretzky or Charles Barkley?

I know this was a long chapter in this book, because it is perhaps the most important of the 10 C's to ensure your success. I hope this opportunity to learn about how people create confidence will assist you in those same efforts.

CHAPTER 9

THE 7TH C: CONTROL

Control (n): authority or ability to manage or direct.

As defined, "control" is that one concept we either long to manage or fear its implications. I freely admit that it is the one "C" that often proves challenging. This goes back to the mechanics we discussed in the last chapter: things we have to do if we are to be successful. The following quote is one I have used for years:

"Order marches with weighty and measured strides;
disorder is always in a hurry."
~ Napoleon

In my stage presentations of *The Ten C's of Success* as I refer to the Napoleon quote, I am noted to say that we all know the type of people Napoleon describes as he references disorder. Some people are always a mess—late for their appointments, putting everything off to the last moment, making excuses for their failures, rushing around like the Mad Hatter in *Alice in Wonderland*. The inverse of disorder, of course, is order. As you observe very successful people, you recognize an order to their existence. They are most likely as busy as you, but are more intentional, deliberate and organized; thus more proactive and productive.

The big difference is how successful, ordered people, manage to handle everything without pulling their hair out or appearing constantly winded and out of sorts. It all comes down to preparation and organization.

Many years ago while watching my daughter, Amy, compete in AAU basketball, I paid special attention to how the best teams ran every aspect of their programs from their pre-game warm-up down to how they wore their pre-game warm-up uniforms. Organized and prepared: the best teams came in prepared with a process, a system. Less prepared and disorderly teams were intimidated by the process of the better teams, just because well-coached teams were structured and orderly in their approach to the game. I observed the same scenarios in baseball, football, and in business. The very best teams are proactive, not reactive.

Travis Jewett, the current head baseball coach at Tulane University, used the limited practice time allotted by the NCAA to teach his players about etiquette when traveling and when representing Tulane University. I believe and agree with Coach Jewett's philosophy that players always represent the university (and their teams or schools). As such, every player wears their uniforms and outfits the same way when traveling. At Tulane, every player, coach, and team member not only stands for the "Star Spangled Banner," our national anthem, in pre-game, but they must stand at attention. These guidelines are part of a disciplined and orderly team and training program for success. Some criticized these activities as a waste of time. I, on the other hand, believe that to be a team, we must look like a team.

In my coaching days we adopted the John Wooden formula for success. John Wooden was the legendary former coach of the UCLA Basketball Bruins. His teams won more NCAA championships than any other program in history. At their first practices, Coach Wooden "taught" and "demonstrated" to each and every player how to wear the uniform of a UCLA Bruin. If it was good enough for Coach Wooden, it is good enough for me and young teens. As stated earlier, we adopted this type of consistency in our program. In addition to having an understanding of how we defined success, we discussed how to wear our uniforms as representatives of the school. Equipment or accessories had to have a purpose, a reason for wearing or using; we did not allow decorations.

I recall one practice that my daughter, Amy, started for me because I had a late appointment (yes, I do have a real job). One of my all-time favorite players, Cory, showed up at practice with these socks that covered his knees. I know he probably saw some NBA player with those socks and he wanted to be cool. Well, we were strict, even at practice. Teams will play as they practice; people in business will win or lose in business situations by the way they practice and prepare.

So, back to Cory: Amy tells him he best put on his team's practice socks before I arrive. He did not and when I arrived he had four choices:

1.) Have someone bring the proper socks
2.) Change into the team socks
3.) Practice without socks
4.) Go home

Cory's father brought him his team socks.

As I said, Cory was one of my favorite players. We did not win a championship during Cory's three years with us, but he won a couple of state championships while at Riverside High School. He was the Most Valuable Player in the state championships as a senior. He is also an outstanding golfer and attended college on a golfing scholarship. All of this and, incidentally, Cory was born with one leg shorter than the other!

In addition to learning how to don our uniforms, we spent the first many practices working on our ten-minute warm-up program. It took us over an hour the first time we practiced the ten-minute program. Every drill in the warm-up program was part of our offensive or defensive scheme. By the end of the first two weeks of practice, we could do it in the allotted time of ten minutes.

Why are these seemingly trivial things so important to success? It is because order marches with weighty strides; disorder is always in a hurry. In Stephen R. Covey's must-read book for any leader, *The 7 Habits of Highly Effective People*, his very first habit is to be proactive. One must take responsibility for their lives and actions. The opposite of proactive is reactive. I preach to our teams in my real profession that we must be proactive, not reactive. Until we become proactive with every aspect of our business, we will have disorder. In business, this means we must reach out to our clients first, not have our clients reach out to us. If we are only reactive, that means we are not meeting the needs and expectations of our clients. We are not performing in an efficient, effective and proactive way.

My good friend and colleague, C. Robert "Bobby" Brown, often talks about the three deliverables we can provide our clients:

1.) Outstanding service or quality of service
2.) The best price
3.) The best product (we consider consulting a product for these purposes)

Here is the catch: we can only deliver two of the three. The bottom line is that cost is always a determinant factor in the absence of value.

We choose to deliver service and top tier products (products can be a service, such as planning or consulting). The service can be great, but the price may not be competitive. The product may be a great price, but it may not come with a level of service some customers find above average. I find it impossible to deliver all three, so we generally choose service and a high quality product.

We supplement these basic deliverables by having efficiencies in our operations. The basis for me, and all of our team, is to:

1.) Manage
2.) Delegate
3.) Direct

The companion to control is discipline in everything we do. Whether it is a vocation or an avocation, the leader has necessary skill sets, the ability to manage, delegate and direct. Many top leaders know that we manage processes and systems. We do not manage people, we must lead people.

Successful leaders also know how to delegate. We must coach everyone on our teams of the value of delegation. Everyone has an important role, but some roles are more valuable than others. We do not want one of our division leaders doing work that an intern or junior-level employee could do. Or vise-versa. To prevent this, we must also direct. We can be proactive and successful leaders by having a written business plan, updated annually, that includes our mission and our vision.

One of the greatest gifts in my business is the opportunity to visit, listen, and learn from some outstanding leaders. I learned from all of them that goal-setting, organization, team building, and delegation are very important tools and habits for success.

Order marches with weighty and measured strides. As we march and advance, we must keep in mind that success is a journey. However, if our only business planning goals are annual goals, then they must be broken down into smaller (weekly, monthly, and quarterly) goals. The most successful leaders build this proactive process and culture into their firms.

The above concepts and ideas are true to all as part of our skills to manage, delegate, and direct. This is true of everyone in most businesses, whether you are a CEO, self-employed, or someone who is striving for the best possible success you can gain in your position. You need discipline to control what you can, and insight to gain control of what is unanticipated.

Successful people take control of what they need to do every day, planning for what they can and commandeering what is unplanned and unanticipated with confidence.

Coaches and leaders take the time to do what is best for the team. The most influential and successful football coaches in the National Football League, NFL, are the ones who take the most time to prepare. The best business and sports organizations also do this—they create systems for success and can duplicate it, despite turnovers.

These are examples of how controlling the process is everything. You need to invest the time to do it in order to have it work for you in a reliable, efficient manner...remember time freedom, from Chapter 1?

In business, control means having a plan. As mentioned earlier, at our New Orleans-based firm, we have a business plan we update annually and we monitor our success. Every January, we invest in a retreat, usually at one of the hotel casinos near us for our eleven-person staff and associates. We get away from the distractions of the office and spend the daytime hours discussing the previous year(s) and what changes we need to make for the coming year. At this meeting, and our weekly meeting, everyone is an equal, and everyone's ideas are taken seriously. Some of our greatest successes have come from what many would think are less influential players on the team. Everyone has the potential to influence, and that we welcome. At the end of the day, we break to have a little fun. Fun is important as we work on our business.

When I present *The Ten C's of Success* in person, I like to ask people in my meetings how many have a business plan. On average, one third of them usually raise their hands. Then I ask them how many have that plan in writing? Many of the hands go down.

I can assure you, having a plan in your head is not a plan. It is an idea. Do not kid yourself that they are one in the same. Plans move you forward and ideas fuel your dreams.

"At 50 you now have realized that getting old is not fair?
And that it is hard to make a comeback when you have
not gone anywhere."
~ John Walter Bratton

John Walter Bratton was a very successful composer, performer, and producer in what are known as the "Gay Nineties," the 1890s. He collaborated on over two-hundred-and-fifty songs. He is attributed to this quote as are others. It was also rumored to be written on the back of a bus as seen in Wickenburg, Arizona.

As I am currently fast approaching sixty years of age, I can attest to the fact that getting old is not fair, and that it's hard to make a comeback if you haven't done anything yet! In our profession, we have a saying that goes something like this: "I have not been in the business ten years: I have been in the business ten times over the past ten years."

Until I learned to have a plan, a written plan, I was a poster child for that quote written in dust on a bus in Wickenburg, Arizona. I was in the business not ten years, but ten times over ten years. I hope, from this day forward, the readers of this book go somewhere. When you do not have a plan, you can be in business ten times in ten years. When you do have one, you can be successful in business for ten, twenty or more years, and you can leave behind a legacy.

Creating a business plan is intensive and hard work, but the process reveals so much, including:

- What you have to do
- Where you need to work on your mechanics
- How and where to gauge productivity and effectiveness

Remember those 1,440 minutes you've been given in a day? Use them wisely. Do not reach the half-century mark and begin to wonder where things went wrong. If you have, there's a good a chance you did not have a plan in place. What is the value of a plan? Let us get back to baseball. If you can't tell, I love the sport on just about every level, but none as much as what it offers kids.

When you are a pitcher, you have to know how to attack the batters when they step up to the plate. The best pitchers know what the batter is going to do because they have prepared for that batter, at that moment. If not physically, then mentally, and through practicing the mechanics needed to have confidence so they could force the batter into an out. Without practice and a plan for mastering what they needed to do, can they be successful? I don't believe so. Batters too. Remember "Stan the Man" Musial from the Confidence chapter? Stan Musial studied the way every pitcher in the league threw his pitches so he knew how they would react thirty feet from the plate. Control means preparation.

The same is true for business. How someone can be successful without a plan is sheer luck; in the long haul, a plan is a necessity. Order marches with weighty and measured strides.

Plans create measurable yardsticks.

Recently I read a book called *The 12 Week Year* by Brian P. Moran and Michael Lennington. The book is not about thinking you only have to work twelve weeks per year, but gives some excellent insights on how you can break down big projects into smaller projects. The take-aways are a great blueprint on how to help people create plans that they can keep moving forward— even during tougher days.

The 12 Week Year purports that we should strive three major initiatives per quarter, and plan and control these initiatives from thought to finish. Science and research has shown that this creates the most balance. The way it works is as follows:

- Say what you are going to do.
- Build a plan and commit to it.
- Build lead indicators and lag indicators (e.g., where you are on target, and where you are behind).
- Create steps on how to get to your initiative.
- Work the plan once you are there.

At the end of each three month interval, you return to the initial measurements you set out to accomplish and ask: "Did I/we accomplish what I/we wanted to in the time I/we wanted?" Basically, you have the "controls" and are the one who can adjust your plan. The key: you have to have a plan. Plans are necessary for everything—work, game, life. There is no reason to avoid creating plans.

> *"Knowing that we can control our own behavior makes it more likely that we will."*
> ~ Peter Singer

Peter Singer is an Australian philosopher and, at the time of this publication, a professor at Princeton University. He lectures on ethics and is an advocate for the world's poor. While you may or may not agree with his point of view, the quote attributed to him is important for this discussion.

If it is to be, it is up to me. That is a saying I have heard for decades. I cannot remember the first time I heard it, but it has stayed with me for a very long time. At the end of the day, we are responsible for our own actions and the results of those actions.

So, if it is up to me that means I control the plan; we control the plan. We write the plan. We write the mission. We have the vision. The result of a written plan is that we can measure ideas and projects. We control our own behavior and thus it is more likely we will. My friend Tim Moreau, the retired CEO from

EDG (Character chapter), with his partners, led his team through planning to create one of the best managed, privately owned firms in the south. Even through the tough times of the energy markets, they controlled their own behaviors.

You know it can be tough to control plans and follow the words and objectives of the plans. When someone approaches us with an idea and we like it, but it does not quite fit into what we need to do at that given moment, having a plan allows us to make such a determination. A plan allows us to dissect what is presented to us to determine the idea's effectiveness. There are many great ideas that we may want to do, but have to pass on at the moment, because the time is not right and the idea does not fit our plan. No does not mean never, it may mean just not at that particular moment. A plan allows us to get to a yes or a no while eliminating the maybes.

I hope my thoughts on the "C" about "Control" are helpful to you. To summarize the main lessons from this Chapter: we must all have a plan for any meaningful objective; we must measure the plan; we must turn reactive actions to proactive actions. Only then can we reach the goals and destinations on our journey of success.

CHAPTER 10

THE 8TH C: CHANGE

Change (n): the replacing of one thing for another; substitution.

Joe Montana was the 3rd round draft pick—92nd overall—of the San Francisco 49ers of the National Football League. He was not the biggest guy drafted, but he became one of the best by knowing how to make changes on the field to move the football. When people would ask him how he was so successful in throwing the football, he would say something about throwing the football to where the player is going, not where the player has been. This is a perfect analogy for change.

Change requires insight, and the best athletes and others are able to tap into that insight to find success in their respective professions. Change happens constantly: it is how we respond to it that is important. Embracing and anticipating change helps us adjust and determines how we proceed on our journey of success.

"Skate to where the puck is going to be, not where it has been."
~ Walter Gretzky, Wayne Gretzky's father

What I love about Walter Gretzky, and his now-famous comment about his son's success, is that it relays the same message about change as the philosophy of Joe Montana. The real take-away from these two examples is that whoever can best manage change is often the most successful.

Here's a personal example about embracing change. About two years ago, our company became aware of a tremendous regulatory change in the financial services profession. Not altogether good or bad for businesses, it was however inevitable.

Many of us fought this rule because we knew it would not accomplish its projected goal. However, with any change, there is opportunity.

The rule is known as the Department of Labor's Fiduciary Rule. In an oversimplification, the Department of Labor, under the Obama administration, determined that all advisors to qualified plan holders (401(k)'s, IRAs, etc.) must act as fiduciaries, meaning acting in the best interests of their clients[*]. Now, who would argue against a rule that states advisors must act in the best interests of their clients? Hopefully, no one in our profession.

Our argument is that the Department of Labor defined "best interests" as basically price and cost (risk and return may also have some consideration). Recall my friend Bobby Brown's definition of value from the previous chapter: an advisor can only successfully provide two of three actions, and price is one of those three. So, if I must use price as a determinant, then I must choose either the quality of the product or the quality of the service to add to price in determining our value proposition. We cannot successfully provide all three. However, change happens and the organized, orderly run organization will best deal with change.

Since our company paid attention to regulatory world, we knew we had two years to be proactive to what was happening, and we hoped the time would give us the opportunity to act as ThoughtLeaders[®†] in accepting these changes.

---

[*] In fact, the Code of Ethics to which I subscribe as a Certified Financial Planner (CFP) and as a member of the National Association of Insurance and Financial Advisors (NAIFA), requires me to always act in the best interests of my clients.

[†] ThoughtLeaders® is a trademarked term of DN Marks LLC

Our goal was to determine how we could succeed in a world of these new rules and to get ahead of others in our space.

We thought then—and believe today—that we had to have a low-cost digital platform on which clients might invest, particularly smaller accounts. With the mandated reduced fees, it became clear that we could not provide the in-depth, personalized service required as part of our business plan for smaller accounts. It was impossible under this new rule to have our full value proposition model. However, we did not want to abandon people we might help just because our world changed.

We began with a projected implementation date on our new digital platform strategy. We had a goal, a destination: to be prepared before the new regulations were in place. It took us a full year, but we achieved our goal. The ruling went into effect June 10, 2017, and we were ready to pivot our business to align with the regulation.

Preparing for and dealing with change is not only necessary for business, but also for our personal lives. In 2005, New Orleans experienced the most powerful hurricane ever to exist in the Gulf of Mexico—Katrina. A name now familiar to everyone, Katrina was ruthless and unforgiving to our fair city of New Orleans, much of which is below sea level. This was such a scary time for everyone, the uncertainty was palpable and at times, almost unbearable.

Hurricane Katrina marked the first time my family and I chose evacuation to ensure our safety. That is how scary it was, as most people who live in flood zones and areas that are hit by hurricanes are stubborn about leaving until they know it's really necessary. With Katrina, too many could not, or would not, leave.

Everyone knows what happened with this hurricane and its devastating effects. What few people realize is that three weeks after Katrina, another powerful hurricane landed on the southwest shore of Louisiana and the southeast shore of Texas—Hurricane Rita. Rita surpassed Katrina as the most powerful hurricane to ever enter the Gulf of Mexico. Within a month, the two most powerful hurricanes ever to swarm the Gulf of Mexico landed on each side of my state.

During this time, our business was relatively young and it was frightening to think what may become of it after two devastating storms. We were fortunate to be located in a place that did not flood, so we had that built-in advantage. However, it was hard to be mentally prepared to deal with so much uncontrollable, unexpected change. It was unprecedented, and there are events in life that you cannot fathom until experienced. This was one of those events.

While there is no escaping change, there is just one thing left to ask: "What are you going to do about it?" You can wait for others to take action and follow their lead, or you can decide that you are perfectly capable of taking some form of control over your next moves and actions.

"The block of granite, which was an obstacle in the pathway of the weak, became a stepping-stone in the pathway of the strong."
~ Thomas Carlyle

Thomas Carlyle was a Scottish philosopher who lived in the 1800s, and what he stated back then is just as relevant today.

My family was in a dilemma about whether to stay in the greater New Orleans area, or to start over somewhere else. The vast majority of our company's business interests were from New Orleans to Houston—the entire region that was devastated. Moving would have been understandable; many others did so for obvious reasons. Yet, when all was said and done, and after a few weeks of debating on a course of action, we discovered that leaving was not an option.

Once we made the commitment to stay, I felt the decision take over inside of me in a most profound way. I knew that the natural disasters that had impacted so many people needed to be thought of as stepping-stones. We picked-up the pieces and used circumstance as our advantage. We needed to help others realize that they could—and must—do the same. This proactive course of action was important to me, both personally and professionally.

Old words from a wise MBA school professor played in my mind: think outside the box.

We are taught in business school that we need to think outside of the box. What I learned through those hurricanes is that sometimes the answer is opposite and may lie inside of the box. Sometimes we have to look internally for our answers. Our action was to state, *Okay we can make this work, and the powers that be are not going to allow New Orleans to disappear. That is not going to happen.*

There was something in my own ability to personally believe that New Orleans could, and would, recover: that was the first step. We all knew and believed that New Orleans, and the Gulf South at large, would return strong and whole again. This belief changed my mindset and empowered and strengthened my resolve. I was able to look at what we could do to be of service to those people who had suffered losses, those most affected who were now uncertain of anything. And, while some advisors in our space and region never bothered to open their doors again, their saying "No" gave us an opportunity to say, "Yes," to adapt to what had happened. We were able to proactively get in front of this disaster and use our actions to our advantage, as well as those of our clients and stakeholders.

We designed some planning programs for our existing clients and potential new clients, and we wrote off 2005 saying it was a "gone year." It was what we did from that moment forward that would matter for our future.

Beginning in October, on Halloween, we sent a letter discussing Katrina and how we could assist our very best clients in recovering from it. Then we set up appointments with our existing and new clients. We were there to help people get back on the ground and back in business, in a sincere and proactive way.

The effort paid off with us having our best year to date. We spent the last two months of the year trying to get out in front of "the puck" and to determine how we could assist our clients with their planning. We supported them by helping them take advantage of the opportunities that would come with the rebuilding efforts, and with Congressional legislation. Everything we did was focused on how we could assist people in their decision-making processes. By starting with our existing clients, and their needs, we found the answer inside of the box by thinking outside of the box.

From everything that took place within our business, we found that our clients and others needed a lot of help and handholding. For me, this is how you deal with change in a positive way.

With confidence.

With control.

You must have a plan, and then make the plan a reality.

> *"The secret of change is to focus all of your energy, not on fighting the old, but on building the new."*
> ~ Socrates

Socrates, the Greek philosopher, is an excellent historical figure upon whom to end this chapter on change. We began with the definition of change as the replacing of one thing for another, and ends with a way to apply that definition to overcome unexpected change. Often, we must fight the old to build upon the new.

Change will happen to all of us. It is how we deal with change that is critical to success and our journey.

CHAPTER 11

THE 9TH C: COMPETITORS

Competitor (n): one who competes as a rival to attain a goal, such as an advantage or a victory.

I have not met anyone who is really good at something who also wasn't a competitor in some way. The qualities of a competitor are undeniable: there's a noted desire for success through every action and the ultimate results of those actions. Self-assurance stands out, and is different than cockiness, arrogance, or the type of ruthlessness that we associate with blowhards.

Competitors seek an advantage and work to gain it. Gaining an advantage is something mentioned in the previous chapter on change. With the two hurricanes, it was my organization's competitive nature that allowed us to seek out proactive and positive change. We knew that we had an opportunity and could turn opportunity into success, if we planned and executed properly. Competitors seek action over talk and bluster.

Competition is meant to be healthy, and the victory is often in what we learn during the journey of competition. Competing does not mean putting others out of business, but instead making all players, teams, and organizations better. It takes discipline and implementation of forward-moving ideas to position yourself or your organization for success.

Competitors are often leaders. They gain advantage by planning, preparation, practice, and creativity. We can compete and achieve by believing in a determination of our own victories and successes.

> *"The true competitors, though, are the ones*
> *who always play to win."*
> ~ Tom Brady

No one can deny that Tom Brady plays to win. Before his career ends, he will probably be the best quarterback of all time. When Tom Brady says true competitors play to win, I believe he encompasses the "play to win" part of that quote to everything thus far written in this book. It means having a plan. It means setting big, hairy, audacious goals. It means making choices, maybe hitting the gym as opposed to hitting the couch. It is about commitment, character, and giving back to his game and his community. It means having a creative plan, which leads to confidence. It means avoiding disorder by marching with measured strides. It means dealing with change. This gives Mr. Brady the confidence of a true champion. However, Tom Brady does not always win his last game of the season. His journey, though, is truly a success.

> *"So many people along the way, whatever it is you aspire to do,*
> *will tell you it can't be done. But all it takes is imagination.*
> *You dream, you plan, you reach."*
> ~ Michael Phelps

When I think about competitors, I find it easy to think of Michael Phelps. In 2008, his successes in swimming, and his competitive nature, led to him setting a lofty competitive goal for himself. He wanted to become the first person ever to win eight gold medals in a single Olympic Games. Many thought he could do it. His toughest race was thought to be the 100-meter butterfly—which was his seventh race. If he won that, it was considered a shoe-in that he would get the eighth gold medal in the last relay event. This was it…his years of practice and commitment for this moment were now in the present. The competitor was set for his defining moment.

The race started and as millions of people around the world watched on television. If you were like me, watching in anticipation and with the pride of the United States on the line; and with those packed in the stands, watching the event in person; many thought he lost. If you were like me, you could sense the disappointment in the air, from whatever place you watched the race. It was still close, though. When Phelps made his last surge for the touch pad in the pool he used every bit of training his competitive nature had for "that moment." That moment proved to be inspiring. He finished with a gold medal, and also set a new world record. He won that race by $1/100^{th}$ of a second!

Think about that…$1/100^{th}$ of a second is insignificant to most of us, but to Phelps it proved to be everything. The years of practice and dedication to working his plan paid off. Yes, he was and is an incredible athlete, but if you do not work on it to become better, what good is that?

This great moment in America's long Olympic history is not only about Micheal Phelps. I think it is another competitor in that race, another American. Andrew Lauterstein won the bronze medal in that 100-meter butterfly by swimming a personal best. He defeated the American, Ian Crocker, by $1/100^{th}$ of a second.

Andrew Lauterstein finished with a time of 51.12 seconds and Ian Crocker finished at 51.13 seconds. To a non-swimmer, that time may seem irrelevant, but to a competitor, it is the difference between a gold medal and not medaling at all. And the $1/100^{th}$ time difference—it is almost impossible to fathom, just a flinch, perhaps, or maybe the blink of an eye.

Ian Crocker worked as hard as anyone. He was an Olympian. He made the finals in an Olympic race. He failed to medal in that race, but would we consider him a success? I believe in all my heart Ian Crocker is a success. His journey led him to the Olympic games, to the finals, and to a fourth place finish. It was certainly not his goal, or his destination. However, success, as we now know, is a journey, not a destination.

A competitor will train endlessly to have the advantage when it is needed most.

When you look at the areas in life in which you want to compete, do you do what it takes to create distinction? Competitors know how to achieve the best of the best by looking at the work they need to do for themselves, and their teams, in order to reach their goals.

Competitors like Phelps and Crocker are willing to work on their mechanics and their performance year after year, spending endless hours just to be the athlete with a 1/100th of a second advantage.

Competitors, by nature, compete. While we see their successes, we do not often witness the preparation, the hard work, and the commitment it takes to ensure success. Think about that next time you see a winner, a champion. It starts with a plan and working the plan. Finally, when the time arrives, the competitor may become the champion.

CHAPTER 12

THE 10TH C: CHAMPION

Champion (n): a person who has defeated or surpassed all rivals in a competition, especially in sports.

Champion is the final "C" chapter of *The 10 C's of Success*. What's so exciting about this "C" is how it encompasses everything that we do both individually and through collective effort, to surpass our rivals and thrive. Whether it seems fair or not, champions do win at what they do. It is not just the glory, but the commitment and competitiveness that allows them to achieve their success certifying that they are winners.

"A loser does not know what he'll do if he loses, but talks about what he'll do if he wins, and a winner does not talk about what he'll do if he wins, but knows what he'll do if he loses."
~ Eric Berne

The insights of Eric Berne, American psychologist and essayist, are refreshing to me. Eric Berne created the theory of transactional analysis—the use of game theory—to discover insight into one's personality. I love the concept of game theory because it uses mathematics and mathematical models to understand the interaction of decision makers. In other words, it's a way of looking at potential outcomes in direct and precise ways.

Also, as Eric Berne says, "The definition of a champion is someone who sees a target no one else can see and hits it." If a champion misses the mark, he or she does not lament the failure, but chooses instead to figure out why he or she lost and take corrective action so that same circumstance will not happen again.

Failure is a key part of the process of success. The very best baseball players, as position players, fail two-thirds of the time. In fact, if a major league position player fails two-thirds of the time, he will be a multi-millionaire. In business, that standard is a little more difficult. Way back in business school at Tulane, what feels like a lifetime ago, we studied what were at that time best companies in the world. This was the late 1980s, the age of CompuServe and before Google. One of the companies we studied was General Electric, the giant, well run, multi-national company of the day. Imagine how many projects were brought to the decision makers at General Electric. How many of those were given resources to proceed?

What I've just described is part of the management process. In our business, my team brings projects (or investment opportunities) to me fairly often. These projects include websites, marketing campaigns, software, and newsletters, among others. It is then up to me and my partners to decide upon which projects to invest. While we have been lucky to have something of a winning streak on important ideas and initiatives, it is important to reiterate that not every project is a winner.

As an example of a successful program, we have an Annual Review Planning meeting with our clients, generally in the last four months of the year. We covered this program earlier. It is a huge success for multiple reasons. First, we know we will connect with our clients at least annually and that is good. We cover a checklist of potential actions, and what is a good value add for our clients. Finally, we send follow-up "Action Plans," thus we have documented the follow-up of all parties.

However, not all projects are winners. We invested several thousands of dollars in a project we thought would put us in front of attorneys. The result was one appointment and zero business. We also tried a peer-to-peer marketing program, and it also failed. We know not every project is going to be a winner, but it is what we do with a program when it is going sideways that truly counts. We choose to fail our failures fast to keep our resources ready for projects that provide a return on investment.

Returning to the athletics example, as we observe champions, we have a tendency to pay attention to all the times they make the winning shot. What we often forget (or rarely have access to) is all the other times that they missed. Champions in athletics and business are those who overcome the missed shots. It is what you do after the miss that really determines a champion. If you miss, are you going to call it quits, or get back to work to better your chance the next opportunity you have to take the shot?

When champions stumble, they:

- Get back up again
- Analyze what went wrong
- Work on getting better
- Wait for their next opportunity
- Take the shot
- Repeat as necessary
- Score!

In business, the greatest of champions have failed over and over again, but they know that their destiny is to persist and remain resilient until the right opportunity comes along. They are not quitters, nor are they failures. It is through preparation and persistence that they position themselves for inevitable success.

Too many people talk about what they are going to do next. Maybe it's a plan for tomorrow, next week, or next year, but they never seem eager to talk about what they are going to do right now—in this moment. In the present is where all champions live, knowing that their actions in that moment are intricate to the outcomes they have in the future. Champions arrive at success through the winning strategy of planning and perseverance.

Champions do not sit around and wait for the right time, they make the most of their time.

Back in 2005, in the aftermath of Hurricanes Katrina and Rita, the reason our business was so successful was chiefly because we did not sit around and wait for someone to explain to us what we needed to do. Katrina and Rita were very difficult and unseen events. What happened was tough, but it was up to us to accept defeat or prepare what we could do to get back on track, and help others do the same.

Earlier in the book I mentioned how I talk with the kids I coach about success, and how it is a journey, not a destination. If we only judged ourselves by winning the last game we would never feel successful—we would never taste it—because we would be disappointed too often. This is important for adults and people in business to remember as well. When we think about the journey, we have the perspective that allows us to see ourselves as champions. It is only from this angle that we can look at success as a journey that can come from overcoming failure.

A championship is a destination.

Winning a title or a race is a destination, but it should not be the determinant of success. It is the journey, and what we learn as we travel, that determines our success. It is the journey that reveals our story. No one is going to win every single time, but the collective accomplishments we achieve, and things we do on the journey, are essential to who we are and where we're going.

"You, me, or nobody is gonna hit as hard as life. But it ain't about how hard you hit; it's about how hard you can get hit and keep moving forward. How much you can take and keep moving forward. That is how winning is done."
~ Rocky Balboa

Rocky Balboa, that great philosopher, is an excellent character to quote as we end the journey through *The 10 C's of Success.* As we do, I recall another great philosopher, Mike Tyson, and what he said after his first fight after his release from prison. His opponent trained heavily and planned well and Tyson was out of shape. Tyson knocked him out in Round One. Asked after about his opponents planning, Tyson said something like, "all that planning is good until you get punched in the face."

Life is tough and hard-hitting. On December 30, 2014, our beautiful granddaughter, Conlee, was given to our family from God. However, she was born with a tear in her diaphragm, something not visible to the medical professionals who attended to our pregnant daughter during her last exam, just two weeks prior to Conlee's birth. The medical professionals did not see the tear or it did not exist. Either way, she was born with her organs sucked into her chest cavity. Her recovery took weeks, but she was released with much love and fanfare from the Neonatal Intensive Care Unit on February 27, 2015. My wife, Cindy, attended the celebration.

At the exact same time, one of our other daughters, Misty, was admitted to the hospital with persistent and acute stomach pains. She was twenty-seven weeks pregnant. Cindy phoned me and told me I needed to get to the hospital as soon as possible. Before I arrived, Brooks was born while Misty was in emergency surgery. It is hard to believe it was the very same day as the day Conlee was released!

Life moves at you fast. Recall what the great Rocky Balboa stated, "life is tough and it hits hard." Sometimes plans go out of the window when life punches you in the face.

Misty had three surgeries in five days and Brooks was in his own Neonatal Intensive Care Unit incubator for several months following his birth. But, fast forward to today, Conlee and Brooks, by the Grace of God, are both two beautiful and healthy children.

And, Misty and Lindsay are healthy, if not crazy mothers. That is life, and it's all a part of the journey.

CHAPTER 13

THE 10 C'S, A RECAP

*"Of course there is no formula for success except perhaps an
unconditional acceptance of life and what it brings."*
~ Arthur Rubinstein

Arthur Rubenstein was one of America's greatest pianists. He
is best known for his interpretation of Chopin. He perfected his
art for over eight decades. His interpretation of life is, in my
opinion, also perfect. We must accept life and what it brings,
unconditionally.

When you combine The 10 C's of Success, you have a formula
that is intricately reliant on each of the "C's," and the effort you
put forth. I can tell you that regardless of what you aspire to do
and achieve, each of these components adds something of value
to your life.

We are people of free will who can make our own choices every
day as to how we are going to proceed through life and the world
around us. Each of us may view success through different lenses,
and this is okay. Our actions will illustrate our dedication to the
outcomes we achieve.

Combine everything you think and feel together with the actions
you take, and it all comes down to time. We all have to ask
ourselves what we want to do with the time we have, each and
every day.

Think of this: if you had seven days left to live, you could think of them as those Saturdays we discussed in a previous Chapter. What would you want to do with your time?

1.) Go to your office and sift through the stack of paperwork you have yet to process or finish?
2.) Attend your son's signing for a scholarship to attend college on a baseball scholarship?
3.) Go to your daughter's last basketball game of her career, and see her make the team's winning shot? Or, maybe to take her last shot, even if the team is going to lose?
4.) Maybe you coach and help others by giving your time to them?
5.) What if that last Saturday you get to see a baby you love leave the hospital to return home to a happy family?

These are just a few options of what is possible if you become more aware of your time, and how you choose to spend such time. As someone who freely admits that I am at risk of being a "workaholic," at least in the way most people define it, I can assure you that managing my time effectively so I can participate in the "Saturdays" I have is a very important accomplishment in my life.

While I hope to continue to grow as a person, I am also reminded of the joy that comes through trying to be disciplined in The 10 C's of Success. These are the takeaways, I hope you receive from this book, and learn to apply in your own lives.

When we reflect back on what we have done, we must ask ourselves if we would rather experience disappointment by the things we did not do, or happiness by knowing that we tried a great many things. Whether they all turned out as expected or not is trivial: it is most important to know we tried.

How will you continue on in your journey, starting now? I truly do believe that if we do indeed shoot for the moon, even if we miss, we will still land among the stars.

AFTERWORD

CONTINUATIONS

Continuation (n): the action of carrying something on over a period of time or the process of being carried on.

This book is not only a testament to all I have learned about success, but it is a testament to my love for my family. A single mother raised me, she worked hard so that we would and could have a chance for success. I think she did a pretty good job.

The totality of who I am today is because of the input, direction, hope, prayers, and help I received from so many others. That being said, it is my hope that this book will help you to achieve all that you can possibly be in this brief time we have on this Earth.

A SUMMARY OF THE 10 C'S

Choices: Decisions are all up to you. You can choose much of what will occur in your life.

Commitment: Decide upon a course of action, and then commit to it.

Character: Your reputation is what others think of you; your character is what you are.

Charity: If you give unselfishly, you will receive rewards.

Creativity: Creativity is what separates the good from the best.

Confidence: Confidence is the result of practice and preparation.

Control: Those who are organized and plan are usually the most successful.

Change: Change will happen. It is how we anticipate it and how we handle it that makes the difference.

Competitors: True competitors are self-assured, not cocky or arrogant. They generally are the hardest workers.

Champion: Champions do all of the things others will not. We define someone as a champion, not by trophies, but by successes.

ACKNOWLEDGMENTS

While I did not write much about her, my maternal grandmother, Amy DeLaRue, is the most influential person in my life. She was wonderful and encouraged me to be anything I wanted to be. I lost her in my early teens, but think of her often. My Amy today is her namesake.

My mother, Diane, and my Aunt Mona are also major influences in my life. I thank them for their love and encouragement through today. Aunt Mona's husband, Uncle Dick, was the father I never had.

As you read in this book, I am very proud of our children. They are all successful and contributing members of society. What else may a parent ask of their children?

Cindy's encouragement in my life's journey is special. There are many nights away from home whether on business; my work in our professional industry; or traveling to athletic events. I know she must wonder how we manage to keep our calendars aligned.

I have many other friends and family who are always so supportive. Many of these people are mentioned in this book. However, our children would not be who they are today without the support of Denise Gillies and Wayne Trant. It is often difficult with stepchildren and stepparents, but their support and collaboration helped keep our families together.

My friends and business partners, mentioned often in this book, are so very important to my journey of success. Mark Cecil and Kim Allen, thank you. My local partners and team, Luke Trosclair, Blake Gillies, Deborah Fortenberry, Paula Soileau, Codi Gaubert, Jennifer Gerarve, Mark Massey, Linda McMahon, Susan Sifford, and Glenn Cedotal, thank you all.

My UWAG family is important as well and are all supportive of my volunteer work as well as growing our national company. Again, there are too many to mention, but our leaders in our affiliates are critical to our success. Bobby Brown, one of my greatest friends and supporters, thank you and Tim Moran for all you do. Ann Baker Ronn and Gil Baker, thank you too. We all miss Golda Baker, who we lost during the editing of this book. Thank you too. Kate Kilgore Cihon and Randy Kilgore, Jon Miliken, along with Roch Ruiz, you are all very important to our success.

My Ameritas family, beginning with JoAnn Martin, our wonderful CEO, thanks you. There are so many who do so much for our firm and for me, it is hard to name them all. Some of this Ameritas family are now close friends, Steve Valerius, Bill Lester, Ryan Beasley, Cheryl Heilman and Bret Benham, thank you for your support as well.

My NAIFA family is important as well. As mentioned in this book, great teams make for success. Starting with our incredible CEO, Kevin Mayeux, I want to thank all of you. Again, there are too many to mention, but I wish a special thanks to Diane Boyle, Michael Gerber, Jen Corcoran, Jen "Money Jen" Cassidy, John Boyle, Sheila Owens, Michele Grassley Clarke, and Diane Powers, thank you for helping lead NAIFA through some tough times. A few past presidents also had and have profound influences on my life. Bob Brown (in this book), Terry Headley, Jeff Taggart, Cliff Wilson, Tom "TC" Currey, John Davidson, Bob Nelson, Robert Miller, and the late great Arthur Abramson, thank you too. Finally, my good friend from New York, our treasurer for years, Peter Browne.

As mentioned many times, I have learned much from my NAIFA Executive Committee colleagues: Paul Dougherty, Jill Judd, Matt Tassey, Cammie Scott, and Jules Gaudreau. Together, we are making a difference on this journey.

Angie Swenson, with the Dicks + Nanton Agency, I must thank for her constant nudging, and sometimes pushing, to get this project completed. Also, my editors, Jill McKellan and Rhienna Guedry, provided excellent ideas and wordsmithing suggestions that I feel are invaluable.

Finally, to Coach Mark Wisniewski and all of our Brother Martin family, thank you for introducing our family to The Miracle League. Watching the smiles on these young faces is a gift from God. Every child deserves the opportunity to enjoy athletics and team sports.

WORKS CITED AND RESOURCES

"Ameritas." *Ameritas*. N.p., n.d. Web. 20 Aug. 2017. <http://www. ameritas.com/>.

Peale, Norman Vincent. *The Power of Positive Thinking*. New York: Touchstone/Simon & Schuster, 2015. Print.

"St. Joan of Arc Catholic School." *St. Joan of Arc Catholic School*, www.sja-school.com/.

Brother Martin | New Orleans Boys Catholic High School." *Brother Martin High School*. N.p., n.d. Web. 20 Aug. 2017. <http://www.brothermartin.com/>.

Lewis, Michael. *Moneyball: The Art of Winning an Unfair Game*. New York: W.W. Norton, 2013. Print.

Kiyosaki, Robert T., and Sharon L. Lechter. *Rich Dad, Poor Dad. What the Rich Teach Their Kids about Money-that the Poor and Middle Class Do Not!* New York: Warner, 2000. Print.

Morley, Christopher. *Kitty Foyle*. Stockholm: Continental Book AB, 1945. Print.
Burg, Bob, and John David Mann. *The Go-giver: A Little Story about a Powerful Business Idea*. New York, NY: Portfolio/ Penguin, 2015. Print.

Warner Bros. Pictures presents a Malpaso production; directed by Robert Lorenz; written by Randy Brown; produced by Clint

Eastwood, Robert Lorenz, Michele Weisler. *Trouble with the Curve*. Burbank, California: Warner Home Video, 2012. Print.

"Show Case." *Daniel's Leather*. N.p., n.d. Web. 20 Aug. 2017. <http://www.danielsleathers.com/>

Carroll, Lewis, and Alex A. Blum. *Alice in Wonderland*. New York: Gilberton, 1968. Print.

Covey, Stephen R. *The 7 Habits of Highly Effective People*. Provo, UT: Franklin Covey, 1998. Print.

Moran, Brian, and Michael Lennington. *The 12-Week Year: Get More Done in 12 Weeks than Others Do in 12 Months*. John Wiley & Sons, Inc., 2013.

About Keith

Keith M. Gillies, CFP®, is the managing principal of Wealth Solutions, LLC and The Pension Center, LLC, and co-founder of United Wealth Advisors Group, LLC.

He began his career as a financial advisor in 1981, with a commitment to providing advice and strategies to individuals, professionals and business owners. Keith wanted to help his clients achieve their personal, business and charitable goals.

Before founding United Wealth Advisors Group in 2013, Keith graduated with honors from Tulane University's A. B. Freeman School of Business with a MBA (1991). Keith also has a BA in Political Science from the University of New Orleans (1980). He is a Certified Financial Planner (1994), Chartered Life Underwriter (1985), and Chartered Financial Consultant (1985), as well as a Registered Representative and Investment Advisor Representative with Ameritas Investment Corp., a member of FINRA/SIPC. He is a leading representative of the Ameritas group of companies.

Professionally, Keith has served as the president of the National Association of Insurance and Financial Advisors (NAIFA), for both greater New Orleans (1996) and Louisiana (2005). In 2008, Keith was elected to the national board of NAIFA, serving two consecutive terms. Keith has served in field leadership with the Ameritas Group of Companies, including chairing the Broker-Dealer Task Force, and as chair of the prestigious Ameritas Field Advisory Cabinet (2010), an elected team of advisors who work directly with the Ameritas group of companies' senior executives to help shape strategies and product development.

Keith holds memberships with: NAIFA-greater New Orleans (Member of the Year in 1997); NAIFA-Louisiana (President's Award in 2004 and the Arthur Abramson Award in 2007). Keith is a life and qualifying member of the most prestigious financial services organization in the world, the Million Dollar Round Table, with status as a Top of the Table member.

For over thirty years, Keith has contributed his time and money to his community. He has chaired the St. John the Baptist Parish (County) Planning and Zoning Commission (1993 – 2013) and the St. John the Baptist Parish

Select Presidential Advisory Committee for Finance (2012). He also served the St. Joan of Arc Catholic Community by chairing the Pastoral Finance Committee for seven years and as the basketball program coordinator and coach for 16 years. In 2013, Keith was awarded the Distinguished Service Award by St. Joan of Arc, the highest of all lay honors. In that same year, Ameritas awarded Keith with the Lester Rosen Humanitarian and Achievement Award for service to his community and to the industry. In 2016, Keith was inducted into the Ameritas Hall of Fame

A lifelong resident of the greater New Orleans area, Keith currently resides in New Orleans, Louisiana with his wife, Cindy and their five children. He enjoys reading, golf, cycling, and traveling with his friends and family.

CONTACT KEITH M. GILLIES

Website: www.WealthSolutionsLLC.net
Phone: (985) 652-7702
Fax: (985) 653-0182
Mobile Phone: (504) 905-1015
E-mail: kgillies@wealthsolutionsllc.net